The hope every leader has is to catapult from being stuck into sustainable motion! This book will help you do just that —move forward — one courageous step at a time!"

Josiah Kennealy

Author of *Debtless*

Co-Host of YoungAdults.Today Podcast

The fact that change can cost you everything makes it a scary subject in most Christian circles. Often, even the word "change" carries a connotation of such negativity that both the word and ideology are avoided at all cost, leaving a great problem. When it comes to the cost of change, failure to evaluate the price of change is equally as devastating as failing to consider what it will cost to stay the same. In 'Catalyst for Change,' Zach clearly articulates this inescapable crossroads and the roadmap for navigating the next steps safely and wisely. Most leaders do not plan to make poor decisions. They simply fail to plan otherwise.

Jon Groves

Director of Digital Billy Grahams

Church Revitalization Consultant

As the lead pastor of the same church (Newport City Church) for the past 11 years, I can tell you that the principles presented in this book will help you in your ministerial and in your administrative duties as a pastor or leader in your local church and organization. Being the father-in-law of the author, Zach Prewitt, I can tell you from close experience that the words he writes, is the life he also lives and passionately preaches. This book will not only give you short term goals to help you succeed, it will give you long term tools to help you sustain. Ecclesiastes 3:1 "For everything there is a season, and a time for every matter under Heaven" (ESV). Are you ready to engage with change and find a solution? This book will help you recognize the need for change and then become the catalyst for the change you long to see!

Rusty Woolum

Lead Pastor, Newport City Church of God,

Newport, Kentucky

In his book Catalyst for Change, Zach Prewitt has managed to lead a new generation of leaders in the right direction and reawaken the successful principles that have long been the reason for success in previous generations. The book is written with wit, honesty, and an authentic voice. If you want to start effectively or finish well, this book is for you. This is your book if you need to change an organization, correct poor performances, or maximize an opportunity. If you desire to change the world into a better, more efficient, sincere, place then read this book. I highly recommend this book for leaders who desire actual change in a world that is literally begging for it!

Dr. Michael B. Knight

Founder and President, The Never Before Project

Lead Pastor, Covenant Community Church,

Madisonville, Kentucky

As a pastor, I am often inundated with book recommendations, especially books on leadership. I have become rather selective in what books I read. I look for books that have a credible author, clear and compelling content, and an author that can get his point across without a lot of fluff. Zachary did that with Catalyst for Change. I encourage you to add this book to your library and enjoy the content that is both spiritually rich and practical in application. I believe this book can be a Catalyst for Change in your life and leadership.

Jason Daughdrill

Lead Pastor, Gateway Church,

Shelbyville, Tennessee

IV

CATALYST

RECOGNIZE THE NEED FOR CHANGE

FOR

FIND A SOLUTION

CHANGE*

ENGAGE WITH CHANGE

ZACH PREWITT

FOREWORD BY TYLER WOOTEN

Fear doesn't have the right to rule us. When we lean into the Lord, He provides the key to overcoming that fear: courage. This doesn't mean that we won't be scared at times. Courage doesn't eliminate fear. Rather, it provides the strength to step over it. When faced with opposition, courage sees an opportunity to overcome. Courage flips the script. Courage writes history. Courage changes lives.

Tyler Wooten

Good Morning: A Minimal Devotion

VIII

Contents

Part 3: Engage with Change

Author's Note

A moment of complete and total transparency. I wrestled internally with this book more than anyone will ever know or realize. As a Pastor and ministry leader, I understand most people naturally anticipate and expect any book that I would ever write to be heavily spiritual and packed with spiritual nuggets. Writing a book has been something I've prayed about for well over a year before my fingers ever hit the keyboard. I, too, expected that when God gave me a word for what this book would be about, it would be deeply spiritual and be rooted in great spiritual truths from the Word of God. So, when He finally gave it to me, my mind immediately started wondering and even dreading the criticism that I knew would come. While this book does have a lot of spiritual implications, and I have not been shy to include Scripture and Biblical truths, this book is also highly practical. I mostly write from the perspective of a church leader and Pastor. However, in reality, most of what I say is usable in any organization, business, or life context. I've simply typed the words as it was downloaded to me. Nothing more or less. That sounds pretty simple, but my mind has been quite the battlefield. I've had to come to a peace within myself and not worry about what opinions of some may be. I know what God has gifted me and anointed me to do. My prayer is that you will read this book and be a better leader by the time you reach the last page. A leader who leads incredible and life-giving change in their family, ministry, business, or organization. You were born to make a difference.

Start Here

Introduction

If I were to be completely honest with you - and I mean

completely honest, I never read the Introduction in books. And

I've read a ton of books in my lifetime. Hundreds. I genuinely

don't know why I'm like this, but I feel as if it's a pretty natural

instinct to just skip over it and want to dig right into the meat of

the book with Chapter One. I mean, there really can't be

anything *that* important in the Introduction, or else the author

would have just put it in Chapter One, right?

Yet - here I find myself, asking you and perhaps even begging you, to start here. Hopefully, you've read the Foreword and Author's Note too, but I don't want to push my luck here.

Don't skip over this part with the hope and trust that Chapter One will start you off where you need to be. In other words, I'm asking you not to be like me, okay? I realize no writer should ever admit this on the first page, but I'm just laying it all out there in the open for all to see. Listen, I know that it may be unnatural for you to start here in the Introduction, but maybe this is a good time to *change*.

See what I did there (wink, wink)?

Let's be real - all of us have been at a place in our lives where we realized that we were stuck and something needed to change.

The office building that I work in has been notorious over the years for its consistently non-working elevator. It's an older building that has been updated over the years, but the elevator just seems to have its issues. In fact, it became an ongoing joke with my previous supervisor and I, because it seemed that every time that she would come to visit my office location, the elevator would always breakdown either while she was there or shortly after.

One morning in my earlier days of starting to work in this office building, I walked into the lobby and headed toward the elevator to make my way up to my office, only to hear the receptionist yelling to tell me that the elevator was down. Great. I do a quick sigh under my breath and begin walking to the stairs.

As I start taking my first few steps up the stairs, I remind myself of something: I literally go to the gym and work out. Sure, no one likes taking the stairs, and only a psychopath would actually enjoy it, but it can't possibly be that bad. I mean, I even do twenty minutes on the elliptical each session at the gym. This should be a piece of cake.

So, I continue on my trek up the stairs. One flight. Two flights. Three flights. And finally, I make it up to the fourth floor, where my office is. And you know what I realize?

I'm breathing as if I'm in labor.

That's what I realize.

Like, your boy is literally dying up in here, okay? I felt like someone had literally knocked the breath out of me, and I couldn't get it back. My face was beet red as I stood there at the top of the stairs trying to catch my breath before going any further.

Thank the Lord that I always arrive to work early and am usually one of the first ones there so no one could see this mess. Shew.

After a couple of minutes, I walk to my office, close the door behind me, throw my backpack down, and slam my body into my desk chair.

I realized then that something had to change. I was miserably out of shape. Sure, I went to the gym and worked out. I even spent a decent amount of time on the elliptical, like I said. But even that wasn't cutting it. I was seemingly doing what I should to stay healthy and take care of my body, but I was obviously still missing a piece of the puzzle.

We've all felt stuck or realized we needed change at one point or another. Whether it was in our life in general, in a job, in our walk with Christ, in a relationship, or whatever else it may be. Every single one of us has been there.

But the question is, did we have enough courage to do something about it?

That's a tough one.

Like, a really tough one.

I realize there will be people from a number of different possible backgrounds and positions that will be reading this book. There will be those who are in the highest level of leadership, those who are at the bottom of hierarchy, and those serving at every level in-between. There will even be those of you who don't necessarily have any leadership role - but even then, you are a leader of your home and of your own life.

Craig Groeschel says it like this, *"What is leadership? Leadership at its core is influence. And the good news is, you have influence! If you have friends, you have influence. If you work with people, you have influence. If you lead a small group, you have influence. If you have teenagers, you have influence."*

If you have influence among people, which all of us do, then you are in leadership. Plain and simple. If this is a new revelation to you and this is your first time grasping this truth, then welcome! Regardless of what your sphere of influence looks like, you have found yourself reading the right book.

I come to you as a man with most of my experience serving in the local church. So, naturally, many of my stories and other things I share will come from that perspective. However, regardless of if you are a lead pastor, laity, volunteer, or staff in a church, or if you are in leadership or staff of any other business or organizational structure, these concepts and principles can be used in all aspects of life - both organizational and personal. In this book, I will use the term "organization" a lot. I use this as general terminology, but you can input what may best fit your situation. For most of you, your "organization" will be a church or some form of religious organization. But, for others, it will be a non-profit or perhaps another type of business. For some, it may not necessarily be an organization but your family that you are leading. No matter what may be relevant to your situation, be prepared to read this book from the lens of whatever that is.

If you stick this out with me, this book will help you to recognize the need for change, find the solution, and engage with change. Again, we've all found ourselves stuck or realizing that something needed to change. The question is, did we have enough courage to do something about it? My prayer is the answer to that question by the time we reach the end and take this plane in for a landing, will be a large and emphatical, "*YES. Yes, I have the courage!*".

XX

Foreword

In 2020 I launched a coaching program for pastors in their 20's. Now only in my second decade of vocational ministry, my heart is to simply give back a few lessons within. Zach was one of the first ones to join this program, although he could've easily been the one to lead it. We began to cultivate our friendship in that context, and quickly I knew that it would move beyond a bi-weekly Zoom meeting and a Slack channel. Having the privilege of coaching many leaders over the years, every now and then you have the honor of catching a glimpse of destiny within someone, and it stops you in your tracks and commands your attention. This is what happened when Zach Prewitt walked on my scene. He is a true student of wisdom, a strategic-thinker, and a man of integrity with a heart to serve without an expected return. He asks questions when he has an answer. He is silent when he could instruct. He shows up when his absence is completely justified. Zach is the true epitome of someone who wants to consistently grow as a leader. This is someone we can all learn from. This is why there was no hesitation when I was asked to write this foreword, and I'm incredibly honored to do so.

A *catalyst for change*. What a thought. What a need. What a calling.

In a society where things are seemingly different from one decade to another, not much has truly changed. There is still great need for true transformation and for leaders to take their place in history.

This writing is a handbook for those who have chosen, not to idly spectate, but to participate in such action. You are reading this today because you are a part of the latter. You're not necessarily looking for *why*, but *how*. You are looking for the tools needed for such a mandate. You have responded to the burden — the call to step up and take your place. As you read this, you will see it all more clearly. You will understand more about *who* you are and *why* you are: why you dream the way you do, why you sense what you sense, why you hurt the way you hurt. You will be able to identify needs personally and professionally, discern the timing for certain actions, tap into the essential mindset for your assignment, learn how to present to the masses with a rally call, and make an announcement to your world that a solution is in motion. You will turn the final page of each chapter with increased confidence and courage to take your rightful place as a leader, a servant of all.

It's vital that we realize that the intent of a Godly "burden" to host change is not to hold us back or weigh us down. It is to give us peace and permission to move. Oftentimes in The Bible when someone had a Godly burden, it was a green-light to be a catalyst for change in that arena. Let's take

Nehemiah, for example. He sat and wept over the walls being in ruin and stepped up to take part in leading the rebuilding process. Was it that he wanted to be known as a top-tiered construction worker? No. It was because of the people behind the walls were at risk. Another case is towards David. What made him confront the giant, Goliath, as a teenage boy? Was it that he wanted to display his slingshot skills? No. It was because the people were also at risk. The burden that they both had to see change was because of people. Our aim in being used in such a way is not so that can become known, make money, or obtain bragging rights. The heart behind it all will always be for the greater good of people: our family, friends, cities, and so on. The people are in waiting...for you.

Zach, from the introduction to the final page, gives us gold that is tried and true. It's easy in a book like this that is so full of wisdom, resources, and content to skim over the words much too fast. I encourage you to slow down to completely consume and meditate upon what is written. As the seasons pass, keep this tool within reach. What a timely book for us all.

Remember that the problems that you see might just be your permission slip to be a catalyst for change.

Tyler Wooten

Pastor, Author, Leadership Coach

Part 1

Recognize the Need for Change

One

Can You See It?

Anytime my family is on an extended road trip that consists

of being in the car for most or all of the day, at some point, we

usually end up playing the ABC game. For those of you who

aren't familiar, I'll explain:

The way you play the ABC game is to be watching for

business signs, billboards, and anything else outside of your

vehicle that may have words on it. Going in alphabetical order,

you try to find words that start with each letter. So, everyone

starts with the letter "A" and you move forward once you have

Part 1

found a word that starts with "A." The goal of the game is to be the first person that gets to letter "Z" and finds a word starting with it. If you're the first one to get to "Z" and find a word that starts with "Z," you've won the game!

Although it's a fun game, it actually isn't as easy and quick as you think it would be. Turns out, there really aren't that many words that start with "X" and not nearly enough hospitals are out there advertising their state-of-the-art X-Ray machines. Weird.

Nonetheless, I love playing the ABC game! It really is a great way to pass the time, and more than that, I'm pretty good at the game. All I'm saying is that 20/20 vision comes in clutch when you're speeding down the interstate while trying to decipher the words on billboards on the total opposite side.

My wife, Sarah, on the other hand, doesn't enjoy the game quite as much. Don't get me wrong - she enjoys the game, and usually starts off with high hopes and ambition of being the champion. But, love her heart, she has terrible eyesight and is too stubborn to get glasses or contacts (she's going to love this part of the book! Haha). I can generally tell when she is starting to be "done" with the game when she starts whispering in my ear asking me for help.

I wish I could tell you that I was a good husband who supported my wife and helped her out, but I regress. I'm out to win this thing, are you kidding me?! I can't help my opponent catch up - how ridiculous!

As can be expected, Sarah's poor eyesight puts her at a great disadvantage in the game. If everyone had equal vision, it would be fair game. But, because our vision is different - some greater or lesser than others - it puts some at a greater chance of winning and others at a much less chance of winning.

Where I am able to identify what a billboard says from further away and continue my search for other billboards, Sarah often has towait until we are nearly directly upon the billboard to be able to read it.

Here's the thing - you can never identify something you can't see.

Part 1

My wife can try her best to identify what the billboard says that I'm looking at, but no matter how hard she tries, she just can't. It's usually seconds later before she is able to see what I'm seeing. And in a game like that - seconds could mean everything!

Again, you can never identify something you can't see. And you won't change something you can't identify as a problem.

In order to ever change, you first have to be able to identify and recognize the need for change.

Can you see it?

The old saying goes, "if it's not broke, don't fix it". If you see no need to change anything, you very simply won't. Why would you? But once you are able to recognize the need for change and identify that something isn't working, you can then begin to move toward a solution.

Identifying the Need for Change

In this next section, I want to help you identify some key triggers that may indicate change is needed. It's going to be important that you come into this with an open heart and mind to receive what I'm trying to lay down. Begin thinking about your context and evaluate if any of these points apply.

Poor Performance

This may be a phrase that's tough to swallow and one you may quickly want to discard as a possibility for you or your organization. However, it's not always as harsh as it may seem. Hear me out:

In order to ever change, you first have to be able to identify and recognize the need for change.

Poor performance doesn't necessarily have to mean that you are nearly in a deficit or performing at a rate that you would be embarrassed for others to see. While this may be the case, it can also mean that performance simply isn't where you would like it or expected it to be.

Part 1

Any good leader is going to set growth expectations over a course of time and set a vision for where the organization is going. After all, *"where there is no vision, the people perish"* (Proverbs 29:18). As a leader, both you and those you are leading must know what the expectations are. If there are no expectations, then literally anything and everything is satisfactory!

It's not uncommon for certain goals to be unmet. In fact, if you have been in leadership for any length of time, you have probably discovered that *many* of your goals weren't reached in the timeframe you hoped they would be.

This doesn't make you a bad leader. A bad leader doesn't even set a vision or goal. A bad leader just wings it from day to day and hopes by some miracle that things work out. In this case, not only are you doing a great disservice to yourself and the organization, but you are being neglectful of the fact that there are individuals who have chosen to come under your leadership because they believe in you and the organization that you lead.

Listen - it's okay if you don't meet goals, and performance isn't what you would like it to be.

Shew. Take a breather on that one! Relax. It's okay.

The fact that you aren't performing at the peak you had set isn't your problem. Your problem is that something probably needs to change. You just have to determine what that *something* is.

Maybe the goal and timeframe you had weren't attainable, or perhaps there is something that is causing you not to be able to hit them. Regardless, very simply, something needs to be changed.

One quick trigger that should indicate to you that there is poor performance within the organization is the increase of and continued allowance of inefficiencies. An inefficiency is anything that causes you not to achieve maximum performance. It is wasting or failing to make the most and best use of resources. To be clear, there will likely always be some degree of inefficiencies. If you are operating at one-hundred-percent at all times, I have a list of Fortune 500 CEO's that would probably love to sit down at Starbucks with you and pick your brain!

Realistically speaking, there are going to be flaws. No one is perfect. No system or structure is perfect. And quite frankly, advancements come so quickly in the twenty-first century that you could be operating with the top of the line today and be old news by tomorrow. Let's just be real.

The problem occurs when we are consistently running on half a tank or less, whether it be within certain departments or areas of the organization or within the organization as a whole. If you know it's always a problem, your team knows it's always a problem, the guy down the street knows it's always a problem…. Well, you get the point. It's a problem.

Your job as a leader is to be able to recognize these inefficiencies that are happening and do something about it. Oftentimes, it is the inefficiencies that become the root cause of poor performance, as well as what we are going to talk about next.

Low Morale

It usually doesn't just happen overnight. Low morale is generally a state of mind that takes an extended time to develop in individuals. You could be seeing this among your staff, volunteers, or members. There is a reason for this, and figuring out what it is will be crucial to the future of your organization.

I was recently in a conversation with an employee of a company that I'm very familiar with and work closely with in our community. She has been with the company for a number of years and has graduated with a Master's Degree in order to be 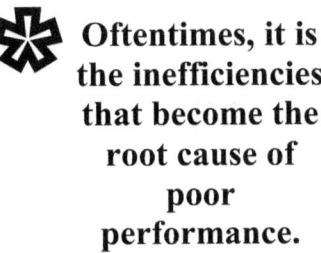 **Oftentimes, it is the inefficiencies that become the root cause of poor performance.** in the position that she's currently in. It's a position she has a great heart for and loves doing.

During our conversation, she began complaining about how poorly her company treats its employees and that receiving a raise or bonus was nearly unheard of within the company. She hadn't received either in years. She had high hopes, though, in a recent company-wide meeting where they said they were going

Part 1

to increase the salary of everyone in her position by $3,000 a
year! Wow! This is great!

Only to be told later on in the meeting that they would also be
taking away a $3,000 incentive the company offers.
In essence, nothing changed.

They gave $3,000 in salary increase but took $3,000 away in
incentives.

It was a wash.

Being knowledgeable of many of the employees in this
company, I can attest with this lady that morale is very poor. In
fact, one day I even overheard a group of new hires complaining
on their first week about how they had been told by other
employees of how poorly the company compensates.
This is not good for the company. It's devastating for morale.

You can't expect people to stay out of loyalty or obligation because they simply won't. Others may stay longer, but most will leave. Whether it's easy to swallow or not, they honestly probably have a right to.

Again, there is something that has caused low morale over the course of time - months and years - and it's been allowed to continue and fester. Low morale is not something that can be ignored. Its cause must be investigated and corrected.

Furthermore, have the courage to ask the question, "Is it me?". It doesn't mean that you're a bad leader, but could it be that you aren't leading the people with the excitement, clarity, and vision that they need? Even if you *are* excited, do they *see* you excited? Do your team, staff, and members know and feel how excited you are about where the organization is headed? If not, they eventually perish.

The last thing you need is for other staff, volunteers, or members to be talking to those who are visiting or newer to your organization about how many problems there are. Not only does this magnify the fact of there being a major morale problem, but you can guarantee those visitors or newbies won't be sticking around for much longer!

You will never experience any significant growth if

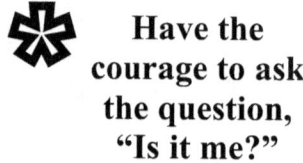 **Have the courage to ask the question, "Is it me?"** there is a morale problem. You may gain a few here and there, but you'll probably lose as many as you gain. It would be better for you to install a revolving door in the front of your building than try to grow an organization full of low morale.

Sometimes, it is a very major issue that should have been resolved, and you may have even known about it. Other times, it could be something as small as a disloyal staff, volunteer, or member that is causing strife. It could very easily not even be your fault that you didn't know it or recognize it until it was too late. But it will also be your fault if you don't correct it. Do whatever it takes to figure out what is causing the problem, and fix it as quickly as possible. The future of the organization depends on it.

Unused Opportunities

In smaller organizations and particularly smaller churches, this is typically one of the top areas where change is needed.

Now let me preface this, along with everything else that I say in this book: in regards to those who are leading in the Church or rely on the leading of the Holy Spirit - the Holy Spirit needs no help. Nothing that I say is meant to override or replace the Holy Spirit's authority and trusting Him through prayer to lead you and to move. Instead, this book is full of practical teachings that will help you to lead as the Spirit permits you to do so.

With that being said, there are opportunities all around us that are often left unused.

New technology. New resources. New ideas. New training. New curriculum. New programs. New systems.

The list could go on and on.

Part 1

Many times, the reason for lack within an organization is because we aren't taking advantage of opportunities that have been placed before us. Sometimes things need to be changed simply because it's time for things to be changed. Any thriving organization will tell you that they weren't afraid to change certain things, as long as it fit within the parameters of their Core Values.

If it causes you to abandon ship with who you are as an organization, that's not the direction you need to go. Instead, the change you lead should *enhance* your Core Values, Mission, and Vision. Change should cause you to *complete* your Mission and *reach* your Vision better and more efficiently.

Don't miss out on unused opportunities because you are afraid of change.

In addition, there are likely unused opportunities even within your staff, volunteers, or members that are lying dormant and not being used. You have people placed before you that are already working alongside you within your organization that have incredible gifts and talents to do wonderful things, but they are being left untapped.

How well do you really know the individuals among you and what they are capable of? And what are you doing to develop them as leaders who can make a difference?

Is it possible that some

If it causes you to abandon ship with who you are as an organization, that's not the direction you need to go.

of the answers to your frustrations and areas of lack within your organization could actually be solved by rolling back the dusty carpet of some of your team members and letting them shine?!

Could it be that you have already been given the hands, feet, and brainpower to reach the goals of your organization this year? All you have to do is let them walk in the gifts they have been given!

Often times the reason people don't let their gifts shine in certain environments is that they don't feel free or inspired to do so. As a leader, one of the greatest fulfilments you might possibly ever experience is giving someone the permission, freedom, and inspiration to use their gifts and watch them shine as they operate in doing what they love!

Take note of this: your organization will never operate at its fullest potential unless all of your team members are operating at theirs. If your team members are suppressing some of their greatest gifts and talents and only giving you the portion you asked for, you are missing out on the blessing that has been given to you.

Your organization will never operate at its fullest potential unless all of your team members are operating at theirs.

Encourage your team members and inspire them to give it their all every single day. Remind them how impactful their work is to the organization and how they are making a difference. Leave room for them to explore new ideas and expand their horizons. Give grace when it doesn't work out, and give praise when it does. Don't be like my wife, who is too stubborn to get glasses or contacts, knowing that she needs them but doesn't want to do anything about it.

Take an honest assessment of where your organization stands from every single angle. In some areas, things may be great. Other areas, not so great. It's okay. Being able to identify the need for change is the first step.

Do you remember the story I shared at the beginning of this chapter about the ABC Game? There was one thought that I threw in there unintentionally just trying to tell a story, but it actually holds significant truth. Here's what I said:

If everyone had equal vision, it would be fair game. But, because our vision is different - some greater or lesser than others - it puts some at a greater chance of winning and others at a much less chance of winning.

The truth of the matter is that every individual and organization have a different level of vision. Some can see things much clearer and quicker than others. While some leaders have the ability to look ahead and see what's coming, others have a much more difficult time anticipating it. Obviously, I'm no longer talking about literal eyesight here, like I was in the story earlier.

Part 1

As a leader, you need other leaders surrounding you who have good vision. You will have a much greater chance of success if you will put leaders around you who can see. If your teams can't see it, you'll never seize it. In essence, you're probably not going to win the ABC Game, and you're certainly not going to level up the organization in the way you would like.

Teams full of high-performing and high-caliber individuals will give you high performance and high- caliber results. Teams full of medium-performing and medium-caliber individuals will give you medium performance and medium-caliber results. Teams full of low-performing and low-caliber individuals will give you low performance and low- caliber results. The math is simple. This isn't to discount or remove individuals on your teams that have trouble with seeing what's ahead, but it does perhaps mean that more training and vision casting is needed. Often times, someone isn't low performing just because they are lazy. They are often low-performing because they don't have the resources, knowledge, or training to carry out the action, task, or function at a level any greater than what they currently are. You probably wouldn't have asked them to join your team if they didn't have the capability to help you lead the organization forward.

As a leader, it's our responsibility to make sure the basic needs are being provided to our teams. Success cannot be expected if your teams haven't first been set up for success by its leader. If you

As a leader, you need other leaders surrounding you who have good vision.

want successful results, make sure your teams have been given the tools to build success.

If you've made it this far with me in this adventure, I must say that you're already doing pretty well. Hopefully, you are taking mental and physical notes of some key trigger points that indicate change may be needed. We still have so much to cover! Are you ready?

Let's keep it moving.

Part 1

Two

Dig Deeper

Have you ever found yourself just asking the question,

"why?" either to God, a friend, family member, or maybe even just to yourself?

Why am I going through this in my life right now?

Why can't I get my team on board?

Part 1

Why do I struggle with having the motivation to do certain things?

Why do my employees or co-workers have to be the way they are?

Why aren't things going like I had thought they would?

Why?

We've all asked ourselves that question a time or two in our lives.

We've all felt stuck or realized we needed change at one point or another. Every single one of us has asked ourselves the question, "Why?" and we've realized in that moment that we were stuck and we wanted change. We were not satisfied with the way things were. We've all been there.

But the question is, did we have enough courage to do something about it?

It's in the moments of asking yourself "why?", that you actually discover your *Why*.

In other words, when you are asking yourself, "Why?" - to whatever it may be - you often realize the need for change, and you *discover* your *Why* and your reason to push yourself towards something better.

And you will never be satisfied in this life until you figure out why you are doing what you are doing.

Why do you get up and go to work in the morning?

Why do you say the things you say?

Why do you do the things you do?

Part 1

You will never be able to progress into a better version of who you are today, unless you first discover your *Why*.

The greatest person of all mankind, Jesus Christ, knew exactly what His WHY was.

Isaiah 61:1-3 says,

> *"¹The Spirit of the Lord God is upon Me,*
>
> *Because the Lord has anointed Me*
>
> *To preach good tidings to the poor;*
>
> *He has sent Me to heal the brokenhearted,*
>
> *To proclaim liberty to the captives,*
>
> *And the opening of the prison to those who are bound;*
>
> *²To proclaim the acceptable year of the Lord,*
>
> *And the day of vengeance of our God;*
>
> *To comfort all who mourn,*
>
> *³To console those who mourn in Zion,*
>
> *To give them beauty for ashes,*
>
> *The oil of joy for mourning,*

The garment of praise for the spirit of heaviness;

That they may be called trees of righteousness,

The planting of the Lord, that He may be glorified."

Jesus knew why He had been called to this Earth. He knew that he had to preach good tidings to the poor, heal the broken-hearted, proclaim liberty to the captives, proclaim the acceptable year of the Lord, and to comfort those who mourn.

In the moments that you are evaluating your organization - and even yourself - and determining areas for change, you must also have the courage to dig a little deeper and begin asking yourself hard questions. You have to discover and know why you do what you do.

In 1666, there was a great fire that destroyed and leveled London, including the St. Paul's Cathedral. Famous architect, Christopher Wren was hired to rebuild the great cathedral that once stood. As it happens, one day in 1671, the rebuilding of the cathedral is in progress and Christopher Wren sees three bricklayers on a scaffold. One was crouched over, one half-standing, and the other standing tall, working very hard and diligent. He goes up to the first bricklayer and asks the question, "What are you doing?" to which the bricklayer replied, "I'm working." The second bricklayer, responded, "I'm building a wall." But the third brick layer, the hardest working of them all, the future leader of the group, when asked the question, "What are you doing?" replied with a gleam in his eye, "I'm building a cathedral to The Almighty."

The third bricklayer was the only one who really got it. The others were just there to perform a job and do what they must to get through the day. But the third bricklayer knew what his mission was. He knew what his purpose was. His purpose wasn't to lay bricks all day; it was to build a cathedral to The Almighty!

It will bring no benefit to yourself or your organization to try and change something if you don't truly understand and know why you are doing what you are doing in the first place.

I realize that there are many leaders out there who know what their *why* is, but there are also a lot who don't. The reality is that a lot of leaders have been leading for so long, doing the same thing day after day, that they have forgotten their why. Leading has become mundane and dull. It's almost as if the vision is there, but it's in black and white and they are waiting for the 1950's to get here so they can see it in color. It's there, but it just needs new life breathed into it.

Simon Sinek says, "*the WHY is the purpose, cause or belief that drives every one of us*".

German philosopher Frederick Nietzsche said, "*He who has a why can endure any how*".

If you know *why* you are fighting, pushing forward, not giving up, not backing down, and refusing defeat, then you will be able to endure any question of *how* that comes your way. If your *why* is important enough to you, then it doesn't matter what the *how* is.

 The reality is that a lot of leaders have been leading for so long, doing the same thing day after day, that they have forgotten their why.

Part 1

If you are willing to give up, then it's not your real *why*.
You need to go back to the drawing board and start asking hard
questions again. The answer you came up with wasn't your real
why.

Questions to Ask

Here are some thought-provoking questions that will hopefully
get your brain going a little bit and will help you better
determine what your *why* is. Even if you feel that you are aware
of what your why is, keep reading and be sure not to skip over
the rest of this chapter. We still have so much more to dig into!

1. What are my values?

One of the most important questions you could ever ask yourself
and determine is, *"what are my values?"*. You absolutely need
to know what's important to you. What matters the most to you.
We all have them to one degree or another.

As a leader, you need to know the Core Values for both
yourself and your organization.

Here is something crucial to recognize: your personal Core Values and your organization's Core Values must reflect one another.

"Now hang on a second, Zach", I'm sure you are thinking right now, "How can you tell me that my personal core values have to line up with the core values of the organization that I work for?"

You are probably thinking about how your work and personal life are two totally different things, right? I would mostly agree with you. Your personal and work life most certainly need to have their separations. That's completely healthy. However, when it comes to your core values - your fundamental beliefs and principles that guide and dictate how you live and make decisions - they must reflect the core values of the organization that you work for, serve, or are a part of in any way.

If they don't, you will eventually be left with a decision to do one of three things: compromise your personal core values, compromise your organization's core values, or leave the organization.

Part 1

It may not happen in the first week, month or year in your organization, but eventually it will happen. There will come a moment where a decision will have to be made. Do you compromise your personal core values? Do you compromise the organization's core values? Or do you leave the organization?

To be clear, in this instance, I am talking specifically about those who are leading in the organization. If you hold a top-tier leadership position within the organization or serve closely in any way, you will likely come to a place at some point where a decision must be made. If your particular context is within a local church or any type of religious organization/ministry, your core values must *always* line up with the organization's core values if you are leading or serving in any way, without exception. Again, there will come a time where compromise will have to happen if they don't.

This is why it's important to know what's important to you and what your core values are.

2. What motivates me?

We all have something that pushes us to get up every single day and do the things that we do. We all have something that we are passionate about and love. Discovering what those motivations are will be a driving force.

For a pediatric physician, caring for sick children and seeing them come in sick but leaving healthy is probably a great motivation for them every day.

For a mechanic, using their knowledge and skillset to repair and fix cars for people is likely a great passion and motivation.

For an English teacher, being able to educate others on how to read and write in the English language and to grow in their learning is probably a passion and motivation.

For the pastor or minister, seeing people surrender their life to Jesus Christ as their Savior should no doubt be a passion and motivation.

Part 1

The list could go on for days, but you get the point.

What excites you?

What gets you giddy inside and gives you a rush that you can't
wait to experience again?

What's your motivation?

3. What sentence do I want to define my life?
This is kind of a tough one. But really think about it. If you could
pick one sentence for people to say about you at your funeral as
they stood over your casket, what would they say?

"One thing that I know to be true about (your name), is they

_____ *"*

How they fill in that blank is genuinely left up to no one but
yourself. Now, let me be very clear that we cannot let others
define who we are. Our identity is in Christ. But nonetheless, we

will be known on Earth by others for the life we lived. Would you prefer it be known for making a difference in the world? Absolutely!

So, how do you want your life on Earth defined? Once you can answer that, you'll find your *why*!

Asking *why* with Change

Once you have a true and deep understanding of what your *why* is, and you have both your personal and the organizations core values engrained in your heart, you then can start digging deeper into the true heart behind leading change.

You've identified and recognized that there is a need for change based on what we discussed in the previous chapter, but let's get the excavator out and start digging into some more questions for ourselves. These questions will have to be asked on a more personal level and also on an organizational level.

Let's get to digging.

1. What causes *you* to identify it as a need?

Part 1

Why is it that you look at something, identify it as an issue, and label it as something that needs to be changed? Is it because there is truly something that is not operating like it should, as discussed previously?

What is your heart behind the change? Are you wanting change because it will somehow benefit you or a particular individual, or is it for the betterment of the organization as a whole? Your desire for change must always come from a posture of having a heart for the house you are serving!

Philippians 2:3-4 says,

Let nothing be done through selfish ambition or conceit, but in lowliness of mind let each esteem others better than himself. Let each of you look out not only for his own interests, but also for the interests of others.

Leadership isn't only about you. Don't get me wrong; there are times in life that things *can* be about you. But, when you're leading others, it will be about someone else far more often than it will ever be about you. As a leader, being a catalyst for change isn't about moving a personal agenda forward; it's about moving the organization forward as you protect its core values, mission, and vision.

Again, ask yourself why you identify it as a need. What will the end result be of making the change? Will the organization be in a better position than it is currently? How will this affect your teams? Members? Volunteers? Those who may join your organization at a later time?

John Maxwell once said, *"There's a fine line between motivation and manipulation. Manipulation is when I lead you for my advantage. Motivation is when I lead you for your advantage."*

As leaders, we have to ask ourselves why we are trying to lead individuals. Certainly, in most circumstances, you are leading someone because it is out of both your and their advantage. However, that fine line cannot be crossed where we are leading people out of our own

Being a catalyst for change isn't about moving a personal agenda forward, it's about moving the organization forward.

advantage more than their advantage. At that point, it becomes manipulation instead of motivation. Ultimately, at the end of the day, it's about us as the leader getting to serve and lead them rather than them serving us.

2. Do others also see the need for change?

When you are leading change, it is often much easier to see clearly for yourself why the change is needed. In fact, many times it is quite obvious to us why something needs to change. But do others within your organization also identify it as something that needs to change? Why or why not?

You will do yourself a great favor to always ask for input from others within your organization before moving forward with change. Especially from the ones that will be most affected by the change. There will be those who have insight that you may not have simply because they are more familiar with the operations surrounding the area of change.

If you are preparing to lead change, make sure that you understand all aspects of what you are looking to change. If you're not careful, you can lead change to make one thing better but another thing worse. For example, you may be initiating a change that will make one person's job easier, not realizing that it also makes another person's job more difficult. There is a balance to everything - and in order for your organization to operate most effectively, balance there must be.

3.   How long has change been needed?

Depending on how long you have been the one leading, this may or may not be a tough one to answer. If you have been the leader during most or all of the time that change has been needed without recognizing it and/or fixing the problem, you likely won't enjoy admitting the answer to this.

Truthfully, though, this question isn't necessarily to bring shame or glory to you - depending on how the question is answered. Instead, it is to say this: many times, the longer that change has been avoided, oftentimes the more difficult it will be to change. The reason for this is because while the issue has continued over a length of time, there have likely been other structures,

> **You will do yourself a great favor to always ask for input from others within your organization before moving forward with change.**

systems, and ways of operating created and adapted that also now work around it. So, because you are finally fixing the one issue, you also have other re-structures that will need to happen.

Let me explain in a church context:

Imagine that you are the Lead Pastor, and you also have a Kids Church Pastor that leads the kid's ministry at your local church. There is a check-in system where a volunteer checks in the kids and a label printer prints out a name badge for the kid to wear and a security label for the parent to bring back to pick up their child.

One day you realize that the printer that is supposed to be printing the labels has been inoperable for over a year and so the check in system hasn't been used either. The obvious solution is to purchase a new printer for your kids ministry and have it set it up with the check in system so that it can be fully functioning again. It's a very simple change, in all reality.

However, now there are a number of other systems in place that have to be looked at.

For one - your volunteer that checks everyone in hasn't had any labels to give the kids or parents for the past year, so now you have to readjust both the kid and parent back to the original system. Kids must wear their name badge and parents must have a security label to pick up their child for safety precautions.

Second - the check in system hasn't even been used in over a year. Does it require any upgrades? Do your volunteers need to be re-trained on how to operate it and what the procedures are?

Third - for the past year, volunteers have been manually keeping track of students on a piece of paper and reporting numbers to the clerk. The clerk now needs to know she will be getting these numbers through the online portal of the check in system again. Does she know how to login still? Does she need re-trained?

There could be other adjustments as well. Again, this is an extremely simple and overall easy change that needs fixed. As easy as it may be, though, you can see how other systems and structures were put in place over time in order to operate around the one primary issue that needed fixed. In your organization, no matter how small or large the change may be, you will likely see the same pattern.

The longer the change has been needed, the more likely it is that other structures and systems have been put in place around it. Be prepared to address these as well. And, in this particular instance, someone needs to be asking the question, "why was this issue never reported?"

There is also another aspect to this question that will lead us down a completely different road. Some people simply don't deal very well with change. As a leader, I have no doubt that you have experienced this before. With that being said, the longer that change has been needed, the more difficult it may be simply because certain personality types don't like change.

This certainly doesn't make them bad people, but it does also have to be considered. You obviously cannot allow your organization to suffer because you are concerned of how certain people will readjust and grow along with the organization. On the flip side, however, it's also important that your staff,

volunteers, and members are going to be on board and able to

help you in adapting and leading the change - not cause more

issues for you.

The longer the change has been needed, the more difficult it

will likely be.

4. What are the repercussions?

To every problem that you may have, there will no doubt be

repercussions to that problem that also have to be assessed.

Because _____ isn't operating as it should, _____ is

happening.

It's the basic cause and effect principle that you probably learned

about back in Elementary School. The solution to fixing the

problem may not be quite as easy, and what you learned in

Elementary School probably won't help you with this one,

unfortunately.

Part 1

Not only do you have to determine what repercussions are happening because of the problem you are experiencing, but you also have to take it a step further and ask, *"what are the long-term repercussions if nothing changes?"*

My guess is that if this question was considered and thought through a lot more often, organizational leaders would be a lot quicker to start fixing problems sooner rather than later.

Typically speaking - the longer a problem festers, the more damage it will do. As a leader, it would be beneficial to have someone assigned responsible for consistently evaluating every angle and aspect of your organization to determine areas of change that were needed and the long-term repercussions if they aren't fixed.

 To every problem that you may have, there will no doubt be repercussions to that problem that also have to be assessed.

As stated previously, you can't identify what you can't see. If you aren't able to look deep and see that something is wrong, you'll never be able to identify it as something that needs to be changed.

As a leader, you absolutely have to ask yourself this question any time a problem arises. Too often, problems are allowed to continue, and generally for good reasons - whether it be because of finances, resources, training, staffing, or anything else. Unfortunately, as grand of an excuse we may have - if a problem is allowed to continue unresolved, it will only grow and create more problems.

Types of Change

Before we close out this chapter, let me leave you with this last bit of information that I truly believe will help you a lot as you work to be a catalyst for change. As you are trying to effectively lead change in your organization or context, you need to identify what type of change you are leading.

There are five types of change:

a. *Personal* - change that needs to happen within yourself

b. *Relational* - change that needs to happen within a relationship between two individuals

Part 1

c.   *Individual* - change that needs to happen within someone

else

d.   *Departmental* - change that needs to happen within a

department or core group

e.   *Organizational* - change that needs to happen within the

organization as a whole

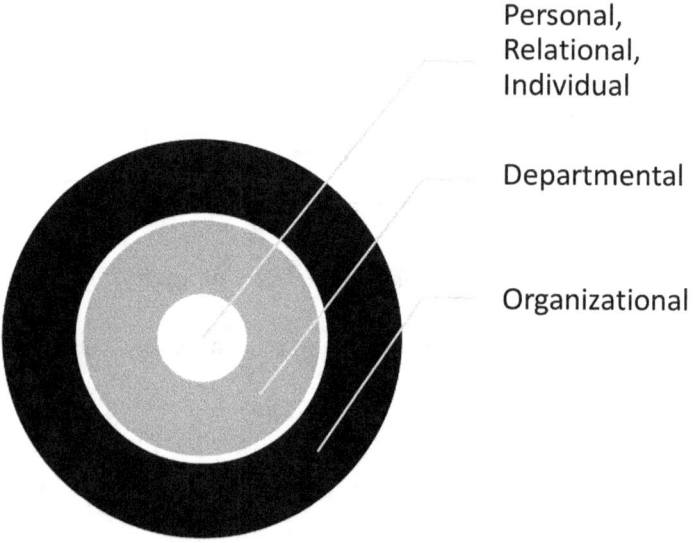

Personal,
Relational,
Individual

Departmental

Organizational

As you can see from the graphic, when you are dealing with

Personal, Relational, or Individual change, it will consist of a

much smaller circle of people - which, in turn, will typically also be much easier to lead change. Departmental change consists of a slightly larger circle and will be more difficult to lead. Finally, Organizational change consists of the largest circle and will be the most difficult to lead.

When you identify a change that is needed, you will also need to quickly identify what type of change it is - Personal, Relational, Individual, Departmental, or Organizational - so that you can begin processing and determining the course of change.

Leading change is a great responsibility and requires a lot of attention and care to details. We spent some time digging deeper into our hearts for leading change, but we aren't finished quite yet. I can't wait to keep digging even deeper as we continue on to the next chapter.

Part 1

Three

Silver and Gold

I have served in ministry since I was sixteen years old, which puts me with about nine years under my belt at the time I'm writing this book. Trust me, I realize there are those who have far more experience than I do, and I respect those who have gone before me. Still yet, this is my story. This is where I'm at right now. I've led a lot of change over the years. It's never been out of a posture of being the new young buck who thinks he can barge in and change everything, though. In fact, I have a very old soul when it comes to what I believe God's standard for living is.

Part 1

For whatever reason, God has gifted me with a business and administrative mindset and has given me an eye to see clearly when there's something that just isn't operating as it should. It excites me to start dissecting systems and structures and find better ways to do things.

You may think I'm a weirdo (and maybe you already thought that anyways), but I would even go to the extent of saying that I think it's fun when I get to fix organizational problems and glitches. It brings me such excitement to be able to recognize that there is a problem, and start researching and finding new possibilities of how we can fix it, and eventually move forward with executing change.

One thing I've realized over the years, though, is that being a catalyst for change will cost you something. Probably even a lot of things. Sure, it's not going to cost you anything like silver or gold (as if you had any just casually laying around anyways), but it will certainly cost you your time, money, resources, and brain power at the very least.

I've learned to start asking myself a question and it's a question that you, too, will have to ask yourself: *Am I willing to fix the problem?*

This may sound like a terrible thing, but there will be times as a leader that you are faced with a problem or made aware of a problem in your organization, and along with everything else going on that you are also having to juggle, you're going to ask yourself this very same question. There are going to be times where you very simply just don't have the mental capacity to be able to handle another problem at that precise moment in time. Perhaps next week, next month, or next year. But, right now, it's just not in you.

Being a catalyst for change will cost you something.

I've been there many times in leadership and I've asked myself that question: *am I willing to fix the problem?* The answer is generally always "yes", but sometimes it also has to be, "*yes, but let's wait a little while.*" And guess what? That's okay! You have to give yourself permission and even encourage yourself not to bring on more than what you can handle.

Part 1

Ultimately, though, as a leader, you must be willing to be a catalyst for change. Again, that doesn't mean you have to start changing things right this very second, and you will probably need to create a priority list of what needs to change now versus what can wait a little bit longer. But, as a leader, being a change agent and leading change is part of who we are and what we are called to do. In fact, if you're a true leader, leading change is in your DNA.

Be the Leader

Most people can easily recognize when change is needed. In fact, if you lead an organization of any size, I have no doubt that you have individuals consistently coming to you with problems that need to be fixed and fires that need to be extinguished. Anyone can walk into a bathroom and see that the toilet is overflowing and be able to identify that the toilet needs fixed. No batteries required to be able to see that one.

On the flip side, there are going to be a lot of problems within your organization and areas where change is needed that genuinely does take someone who knows their job and the organization like the back of their hand, and truly cares. When someone comes to you with a problem they have recognized, it's probably that they are coming to you because they are knowledgeable, experienced and realize that something needs to be done. There is something happening within the organization that is not satisfactory to the organization's core values, mission, or vision. There is something that is performing at less than expectation.

Truly, it takes a visionary to see the need for change. It takes an individual who has the ability to be able to see in their mind something better than what they are currently experiencing. You need a team full of visionaries. You need a team that will always be able to see a better version of your organization, because they will take that creativity and help you develop something greater.

What you have to understand, though, is that someone who is only a visionary can't get you but so far. It takes a visionary to see the need for change, but it takes a leader to be a catalyst for change. It takes a leader to actually be able to lead change and to do something about it.

But you first need to have a visionary before you can ever have a leader. If you have someone who can see a better version of your organization and they know what it takes, you can take that person and train them to take ownership and leadership to absolutely transform the organization and department they serve in. You cannot lead others into a future you can't see. This is why your team members have to be visionaries before they can ever be leaders.

Furthermore, just because they are visionaries, doesn't mean they should be placed in a position of leadership. Not everyone - and, in fact, probably most - is willing to commit to the sacrifice that leading requires. As I said earlier in this chapter, being in leadership and being a catalyst for change will require something of you.

 It takes an individual who has the ability to be able to see in their mind something better than what they are currently experiencing.

It will cost you something. At the absolute very least, it will cost you your time - and I'm not sure about you, but my time is precious and is worth a lot to me. I don't want my time to be wasted, but I want it to be well spent.

Am I Willing to Fix the Problem?

I'm not sure if this question hits you the way that it hits me, but this is a very brutally honest question to ask yourself. *Am I willing to fix the problem?* For most of us, this is a hard one to answer. The reason being is probably because, as a leader, you never want to say "no". Not even to just this question, but in general. Anytime someone asks something of you, asks you to do something, or asks for your permission, you naturally want to be able to give a big and emphatical "YES!". Unfortunately, you can't always do that. And there are times where you simply just can't say "yes" in that particular moment because there are too many other things you are trying to juggle. Again, it's not a "no", it's just a "not right now".

Whenever you are at decision making time and you have to reach a conclusion of whether you can put something else on your plate, the cost must be counted. Literally and figuratively. Yes, the literal cost will have to be looked at and considered - but quite honestly, I'm no financial expert so that goes way beyond the scope of this book. What I'm talking about is the cost of your emotions, time, health, family, etc. How much of your time is it going to take? How much stress is this going to add? Will this take a toll on your health? Your family?

Most change that you lead probably won't be all that dramatic, but other change absolutely will. I have seen churches split and nearly collapse over one tiny decision because people didn't like it. Sometimes it's change that you think will cost you the least that actually costs you the most. Thankfully, though, not all change is major change. Some change will come about much easier, quicker, and smoother than others. You will be able to recognize the problem, quickly find the solution, and engage with change with little to no stress whatsoever.

To be frank, that's not the kind of change that you ever have to ask yourself if you are willing to fix the problem. It's the change that you know will cost you a lot. It's the change that you know will require a lot of money, time, resources, exhaustion, and especially a lot of prayer, that causes you to ask yourself that question. It's the change that you know will not come easy and may even require a fight out of you.

Status Quo

I've become very accustomed to being the one who is always stepping outside of what many like to call "normal", and doing things at a much younger age than many would probably even be comfortable with. Let me give you some examples. I promise I'm going somewhere with this, so please stick this out with me.

- At the age of 16, I started the first level of ministerial ordination process within my denomination and by 17 I was officially ordained. The minimum age requirement is 16 years old, but there were no others in my state at the time and few within the denomination.
- At the age of 17, I was welcomed to the Church & Pastor's Council at my local church to serve as a council member who discussed and handled the finances of the church among anything else relating to the operation of the church. Again, the minimum age requirement was technically 16 years old - but in the 100+ years the church had been in existence, this had never happened before.

Part 1

- At the age of 20, I returned home from school for the Summer and was asked to step in temporarily as Interim Pastor of a church about an hour away until the State Overseer of my denomination was able to assign a new Pastor. Granted, I was only there for about a month because someone had been found- but the Overseer had enough faith in my ability to lead, not knowing how long I could potentially be there.

- Presently, at age 25, I serve with my wife as the Associate Pastor and Young Adult Pastor of a thriving and vibrant church located in the Inner City, minutes away from Downtown Cincinnati.

I hope that you will please hear my heart as you read all of these things, because I don't say them to try to bring any accolades to myself. To be frank, I don't enjoy attention being on me. Ironically enough, I usually despise having attention drawn to myself. Preaching and teaching is different, obviously. But other than that, I do quite well making sure everything in the background is operating as it should.

Instead, I tell you these things because I've always been willing to fix problems that were set before me and I didn't care what it cost me. There have been more times than I can count that I've nearly convinced myself that I couldn't do something because I was too young to do it. I allowed a stigma and opinions of others to start implanting thoughts into my mind that I couldn't do it. I wasn't old enough, experienced enough, or educated enough. There were far more qualified people who were older than me and had more experience than me to complete the task. I didn't have what it took. But you know what I found out? Yes, I did! And yes, I still do!

As a leader, you have to be willing to throw "status quo" in the garbage. People will try to judge your ability by a number of different factors that they think come into play. They will take their judgements and they will either lift you up on a pedestal or they will rip you to shreds. At the end of the day, it's all garbage. What truly matters is that you have been placed in your position not only by your peers, but most importantly by God. You have been trusted to lead your organization. It doesn't matter what others believe about your ability and it doesn't even matter what you believe about your ability. If you are willing to do whatever it takes, that's all that matters.

Status Quo is a fence that will keep you locked up and confined, if you let it. Outside of that fence is where you are actually supposed to be and stay. Too many leaders allow the Spirit of Status Quo to keep them from ever pursuing after something greater. Merriam-Webster defines status quo as "the current situation: the way things are now." There are people who want to convince you "that's just how it is, learn to live with it!". And while the reality of what they are saying may be true, that doesn't mean that you have to allow it to fence you in. As a leader, you have two options:

1. Stay inside the fence of Status Quo.
2. Get the wire cutters out, cut the lock, and bust out of there!

If you are going to be a catalyst for change and truly make a difference in your organization, option two is the only way to do it! You cannot make an impactful and lasting difference in your organization by following status quo. You simply can't. You

have to be willing to fix **Status Quo is a fence that will keep you locked up and confined, if you let it.**

the problem and do

things that no one else

is willing to do. It will absolutely cost you something, but you

have to determine that it's worth it! Imagine what it would have

been like for me if I waited until "status quo" allowed me to do

some of the things that I did. Allow me to help you put it into

perspective.

- The average ordained minister in my denomination is in

  their 30's. If I followed status quo, I still wouldn't have

  done what it took to obtain the first ministerial ranking.

  I'm currently at the second of three rankings as Ordained

  Minister.

- Most of the others on the Church & Pastor's Council

  with me at the time were anywhere between their upper

  40's to 70's. I still wouldn't be anywhere close to

  stepping into a council member role. Yet, I did that when

  I was 17!

Part 1

- According to a Barna Group study[1], the average age of
  Pastors is currently about 52 (as of 2017). Still yet, most
  of the younger Pastors in my circle that I know of are in
  their early 30's. Regardless, I definitely wouldn't have
  been an Interim Pastor when I was 20, and I would still
  be too young to be an Associate Pastor.

Taking all of this into consideration, could you begin to imagine
all of the opportunities, experiences, and growth that I could
have missed out on in my life if I allowed myself to live in the
fence of Status Quo? Living in Status Quo will absolutely cripple
you and hinder you from doing great things in your life and in
your organization.

Speaking of fences, let me give you one more story that may
help you really get a grasp on what I'm trying to get you to hold
on to.

There's a large, shaggy-haired dog that stands just as tall as an
adult human and probably weighs close to the same as one as

well. We'll call him Bailey. Bailey is a good boy. He sees cars

drive by all the time in front of his yard, but no matter how much

he wants to go chasing after one, he never does. He always stays

in the yard and won't even get on the sidewalk when the

newspaper guy comes walking by, or when the two neighbor

boys ride their bikes in the Summer. Bailey desperately would

love to play with them, but he always stays in the yard in front of

his house.

Why?

Bailey's owners have an invisible electric fence installed in their

yard.

Well, actually, Bailey's owners *used* to have an electric fence

installed in their yard. But, ever since a bad lightning storm came

through a few months ago, there's been a short in the electric

fence and so they eventually turned it completely off. Even

though the fence hasn't been on for quite a while now, Bailey

still stays inside the yard and within the parameters of the fence

because he thinks he can't go beyond it. In his mind, he is like a

Part 1

prisoner stuck inside the yard by this underground demon that he can't see. He has no idea that the only thing keeping him constrained is a lie that he has believed to be true.

You're probably laughing or at least smiling at this point, but it's quite possible that you are more like Bailey than you even realize.

Could it be that you, too, have believed a lie and it's causing you to miss out on something so much greater in your life? Yes, something even greater than chasing cars as they pass by, attacking the newspaper boy, or playing with the neighbor's kids. Is it possible that someone has told you somewhere along the way how far you are allowed to go and you believed them? Perhaps it was a lie that no one even told you, but you convinced yourself of it.

My friend, don't settle for Status Quo. Don't allow a lie to be implanted into your mind that wants to put you inside a fence and tell you to go no further. You were created to fulfil a great purpose in this life.

Again, are you willing to fix the problem? Are you willing to do whatever it takes no matter the cost? If you are going to be a leader who makes a difference in your

organization, in those who serve alongside you, and whoever

else may be impacted by you, then you absolutely have to be

willing to do whatever it takes and kick status quo to the curb!

Investing not Spending

Here is an incredible truth that you, as a leader, must realize if

you ever want to make a lasting impact and be a true catalyst for

change who is willing to make sacrifices: as a leader, you don't

spend. You invest.

Every single leader has money, resources, and time

(moving forward, we will lump sum these all into "resources").

While we all have the same number of hours in a day, our

availability of money and other resources will look different.

Merriam-Webster defines a resource as "a source of

supply of support." Simply put, a resource is what you have

readily available as a support to accomplish whatever it is you

need to accomplish. This goes beyond even money and time, and

includes your staff, members, volunteers, supplies, equipment,

facilities, talents, skills, your credibility, your influence, and the list could go on and on. Again, each of our lists of resources will look very different. Regardless, though, if you look at your resources as expenditures rather than investments, you will more likely hold back on how you use them. If your resources are treated as a list of expenses that keep deducting from your account balance, you'll eventually stop once your account reaches a balance that starts to make you feel uncomfortable. As a leader, you have to think of your resources as investments, not spending.

Spending money is a fair trade. You are spending a fair amount of money based on the market for an equal return in a 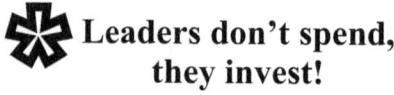 **Leaders don't spend, they invest!** product or service. You expect a fair return for what you spend. But investing isn't a fair trade. Investing is expecting an exponential growth of return. When you invest in something, you expect that you are going to get more in return than what you put in.

Here's the key: good leaders know when and how to make good investments. You can put your resources into something and expect it to be a good investment that will bring you an exponential return, but in reality, it' be a bad investment with little to no return. This is where you have to use good judgement and prayer. A good leader will know what investments need to be made and how to make them. You have to be able to look at your resources and properly allocate them in a way where you are investing for ample return. Some investments will naturally be better than other investments.

Look around at your organization. What do you see? Do you see a lot of flourishment or a lot of lack? Do you see a lot of high performing team members and leaders or ones who have some growing to do? Do you see well performing systems and structures or broken ones? Does the name on the front door of your building have a good rapport in the community or a poor one? As a leader, if you are a stingy investor, you'll get stingy results. If you're not good at properly investing, it'll show. As you look around at your organization, take note of where things aren't where you would like them to be. No, seriously. Take note of them. These are the areas that you have probably historically been a stingy investor and need to deeply re-consider how you are or aren't investing and allocating resources.

Part 1

Throughout my time in the church-world, I've seen this first hand more times than I care to mention. Most churches have an imaginary "Top Five" list of ministries they like to pour mostly all of their resources into. Typically speaking, they are: Kids, Youth, Men's Ministry, Women's Ministry, and Outreach/World Missions. Obviously, these are all very good things to pour our resources into. Unfortunately, though, this means that there's little to no room for any resources to be directed to anything else that's just as impactful. If these five are getting all the resources, everything else is in lack. This is where proper management of our investments comes into such an important play. You're directing resources to these ministries, and that's great, but there could possibly be other ministries that are equally as important and need solid investing as well!

Hear me out for a minute - if you are pouring a ton of resources into your Kids Ministry and Youth Ministry, I think we can all agree that is a very good investment. However, all that money being poured into kids and youth won't do much good if they leave your church once they turn a young adult because there's nothing there for them. I'm not saying that it's the right thing for them to do, but it's still a reality no matter how you may feel about it. You invested in the kids and youth properly, but you were stingy when it came to investing in young adults. And guess what? There's a lack. You were stingy with your investing and you got stingy results. I may use this as an example because I'm a Young Adult Pastor so I'm naturally biased, but I also use it as an example because I know what I'm saying is the absolute truth and happens way too often in churches.

I used that merely as an example to help you better understand the point I'm trying to get across. Again, take note of areas where you see lack or where you wish you saw better performance and you will know what areas you need to invest more into. I'm no mathematician, but this is simple math for me!

Before we move forward, start working on that list. Having it by your side will become very handy as we continue into the upcoming chapters. We are going to take that list of yours and walk through how we can fix the problem and eventually engage with change. Put a smile on your face, leader. You're making a difference in your own life and those around you!

Also, as we close out Part One, be sure to look over and answer the Discussion Questions on the next page. Hopefully these will help keep your brain working and remind you of some of the key points we discussed in these first three chapters.

PART ONE

DISCUSSION

QUESTIONS

1. What are the three triggers to identifying the need for change?

2. What other triggers have you seen or currently seeing?

3. What type(s) of change do you see is most needed in your organization right now (Personal, Relational, Individual, Departmental)? Why?

Part 1

4. Are you willing to fix the problem? Why or why not?

5. What are the repercussions that are being caused because of the problem(s)? What repercussions will happen if it's allowed to continue?

6. What costs (regarding ALL types of resources) will be incurred to fix the problem(s)?

7. Is it an expense or an investment? There's only ONE *right* answer!

Part 2

Find the Solution

Part 2

Four

Alignment

Paul Bloom is the Brooks and Suzanne Ragen Professor of Psychology at Yale University. His research explores how children and adults understand the physical and social world, with special focus on morality, religion, fiction, and art.[2] While he has completed a number of studies, some of his research has been on pleasure and how we experience pleasure through our physical and social world. In one of his books, *How Pleasure Works*, Bloom states that *"Pleasure is affected by deeper factors,* *including what the person thinks about the true essence of what he or she is getting pleasure from,"*. In other words, our level of pleasure is greatly dependent upon what thoughts we may already have about something.

Furthermore, when experiencing something blindly, he found that someone's level of pleasure is based on what they believe it is. He uses an example that those in a study found more pleasure drinking Coke with a brand logo on the cup versus Coke from an unlabeled cup. When drinking from a blank cup, it was probably assumed by most that they were drinking an "off brand" and automatically had a preconceived idea the drink wouldn't taste as good as a "name brand".

Finally, Bloom's book indicates through his research that he has found the more you know about something, the more you love it, and ultimately want to share it with others. Bloom says. *"Knowing more about it, you make discriminations, you categorize things better, and you can increase your pleasure. This is obvious with something like classical music, but I think it is true for everything."*

Alignment

You can definitely see this to be true in far more than just classical music. A good friend of mine is a car enthusiast. He is exactly what you think of when I say that, too. He knows nearly everything there is to know about any given car that is going down the road, especially older model cars. He's the guy that shows up to car shows virtually every weekend during car show season. And, as can be expected, he's the guy whose car sounds incredibly too loud and scares the living daylights out of you as he passes by you on the Interstate. Yeah, that guy. But he is extremely knowledgeable when it comes to cars and he is hands down the first person I go to when I have a car question. If he doesn't know, his dad does! Because of his love for cars, he is always sending me videos and pictures of cars. Anytime we are out together and he sees a particular super cool car that draws his attention, he wants to tell me everything about that car and what makes that car so special. Although mostly everything he tells me is entirely over my head, I don't mind at all because I genuinely just enjoy seeing him so excited to tell me all about it.

I would say that we are probably all like this to one degree or another. We have a particular skill, hobby, or something we are very good at or at least knowledgeable with, and we love when we get to share what we know with others. Not in a boastful way to say, "look at me!", but simply excited to be able to share with others and teach them about something that we love.

All the Love

At this point in time, you're hopefully at least intrigued by Paul Bloom's research, but ultimately you're really just wondering how any of this has to do with being a catalyst for change and finding the solution to the problem(s) within your organization. If you haven't thought that yet, you must really have a lot of faith in me! Which is either really smart or really dangerous. I'll let you pick.

Here's the 4-1-1. If you are ever going to find a solution that works for your organization, you must first have a love for your organization. Having a love for your organization will be an outflow of how much knowledge you have about it and how much the organization excites you to the point of wanting to tell everyone about what you do and what's going on within it. If you don't love it, you might find a solution, but it likely won't be the right solution or the best solution. If you truly love something, you want the best for it. Loving your organization will cause you to do whatever it takes to make sure that the solution you find is the perfect match. You will want to make sure that you find the right solution, because not finding the right solution could cause even more harm.

They key term for all of this would be *alignment*. The solution must be in alignment with your organization's core values, mission, and vision. If the solution doesn't align, it won't work. And if you're

If you truly love something, you want the best for it.

not in alignment, you won't find the solution that does work. Before you should ever begin searching out solutions, you need to make sure that your heart is in a place to do so. Before proceeding to finding a solution, start by asking yourself these questions:

Part 2

1. Do I talk about the good more than the bad?

If you tend to talk about and focus more on the bad and negative

aspects of your organization, your focus is in the wrong place.

To be sure, talking about and focusing on the bad is most

definitely not a bad thing. In fact, you need to do that. But your

heart should naturally lean more toward uplifting the

organization than tearing it down.

2. Do I enjoy my time here? Am I excited about what
    my organization is doing?

If you love your organization, you will thoroughly enjoy when

you get to walk through the doors. You will be excited about

where your organization is and what it is accomplishing. Your

thoughts should be, "I hope I get to....", not "I hope I don't have

to...". This will take you back to my first question, because if

you are excited about it then you will want to talk about all the

good. You will be excited to tell others about what is happening

and what your organization is doing!

3.   Do I think about getting better instead of surviving? A love for your organization and what you do will cause you to want to get better than you already are, not merely focus on just getting through the days, weeks, months and years, doing the minimum it takes to survive. Surviving is not and never will be thriving. Someone who loves their organization wants it to thrive and they want to thrive with it!

You may be asking yourself, "why is it really that important that I ask myself these questions and for me to love my organization? All I'm wanting to do is find a solution to a problem I've recognized. It's really not that big of a deal, Zach." I'm glad you asked. If you don't love your organization, trying to find solutions to its problems isn't the task for you. Not only because you won't find the best solution, but it will also drain you. Hear me out: If you don't like your organization, that tells me that you probably answered "no" to the questions I just asked you to answer. Meaning:

1.   You tend to talk bad about your organization more than you do good.

Part 2

2. You don't enjoy your time and aren't excited about what the organization is doing.

3. You're more focused on surviving than thriving.

Simply put, you honestly aren't all that happy when you're there, you would rather be somewhere else, and you don't have many positive things to say about it. If that's the case, it sounds like your organization is draining to you. Would you like to take a guess at what will happen when you create a list of all the "problems" the organization has and you're stuck with being the one trying to figure out what to do about it?

Yep, you guessed it. Drain you even more.

Not only is this not a healthy assignment for your organization's sake, but it's also putting you in a place that's not healthy for your own sake either. One of two things need to happen:

1. You need to find a love for your organization

2. You need to find someone else who does

It's as simple as that. It can happen to anyone. It doesn't matter if you are the Leader, a Department Lead, staff, volunteer, or member. Going through seasons of drought and feeling drained will absolutely happen. It doesn't make you a bad person or leader, but it does mean that you need to make sure you have a love in your heart for the organization before you begin trying to dissect and solve its problems.

Let me tell you a story to help you better explain my point and hopefully get you to a place of understanding why this is all so important. The other day, I called my wife, Sarah's, desk phone at her work because I needed to tell her something. To my surprise, the person who answered on the other side of the line wasn't Sarah. I knew it must have been one of her other co-worker's, but I wasn't sure who. Since I knew it wasn't my wife answering, I kindly asked if the person could put me in touch with her. A few moments later, I hear another voice come to the phone, and I immediately recognized that it was Sarah's. Although I've met her co-workers a number of times and we all know each other, I wasn't able to recognize whose voice it was that I was talking to. Yet, I knew immediately when my wife's voice was behind the phone. My level of relationship and knowing my wife is hundreds of times deeper and greater than my level of relationship with her co-workers. I have a deep love for my wife and I've spent untold hundreds and thousands of hours with my wife. I could see one facial expression of hers and write you pages on what she is thinking in that moment, that's how well I know her. Because I know her so well and love her so much, I also have a deeper love for her. Certainly, much deeper than the surface level of love I may have for her co-workers, whom I only have a godly love for. And out of my deep love for my wife and my commitment to her, I made vows to her on our wedding day to stay with her no matter what life may bring us and to care for her, protect her, and seek out her best interest in all things. But, genuinely, I don't keep those vows because I have to or made a vow to do so. I keep them because I want to, as a byproduct of my love for her.

When you love someone, you want the best for them. You are willing to fight for them and seek out their best interest at all times. I would never do anything that could knowingly cause her harm or impact her in any negative way. Knowing that she is in pain and is hurting, also hurts me. It causes a deep, inner pain to rise up in my heart. My protective instincts start kicking in. Why? Because I love Sarah.

This is the kind of heart and love that you need to have about your organization. Now please understand what I am and what I am not saying here. Notice that I said, "this is the same *kind* of heart and love", not "this is the same *level* of heart and love".

To say that you have the same level of heart and love for your organization is to say that you love your organization equally as you love your spouse and put them on equal playing ground. This most certainly should not be the case! Instead, you should have this same kind of heart

Trying to lead change and fix problems within your organization without a heart for the house will likely only bring you more frustration and trouble.

and love for your organization. Meaning, to have similar characteristics. You love your organization and want what's best for it. You are affected to some degree when things are impacting your organization in a negative way. You have a great depth of knowledge about your organization and can write pages about it. At the end of the day, you always want what is best for the organization.

Some of you think I'm crazy right now, but I'm telling you that you must have a heart for the house you are serving. Without a deep love for it, your heart will never be at a place to seek out what is truly best and know in your heart that the solution you are finding is what the organization truly needs. If you don't love it, you may eventually find yourself at a place where you are willing to compromise just for the sake of getting to a solution and moving on to something else.

Again, it all comes down to being in alignment. My dictionary defines alignment as being "in correct or appropriate relative positions". If your heart isn't in the correct position, you're not in the correct position to lead change. Please hear what I'm saying from a humble posture. I say these things because trying to lead change and fix problems within your organization without a heart for the house will likely only bring you more frustration and trouble. As I said earlier, it will do nothing but drain you even more and leave you with less in your tank when you had already started on empty. That is not a place you want to be, my friend.

What if I'm not in Alignment?

If you're reading through this chapter and realize that your heart may not be in a place where you should be leading change, this section is especially for you! If you do think you're fine, I would strongly encourage sticking around and continue to read on anyways. You never know when you might be in this type of situation or how you may be able to gain insight on how to help someone else in the future.

If you do feel as though you are out of alignment, you may be asking yourself, "What now? What can I do to get back in alignment?". If you are asking yourself those questions, that leads me to believe that you do still genuinely care and want to change! Most likely, you started out at one point very strong, excited, and in love with the organization you serve. Over time, things slowly changed or perhaps they abruptly changed because something happened. Still yet, if there wasn't even the slightest inch inside of you that cared, you probably would have never

Part 2

picked this book up in the first place. On behalf of those who are impacted by your leadership, thank you for caring!

So - you've found yourself in a place where your heart may not be in a proper place to be leading change. What now? Well to answer your question of, "what now?", I first need to counteract with two questions of, "when?" and "how?".

WHEN?

Begin to think back over the time you have been at your organization and all of the feelings and emotions that are tied to it. As I said previously, I'm sure that you started out on a very high note where you were full of excitement and expectation. When did that change? At what point in time did that excitement no longer linger? Was it one specific event or occurrence or was it something that happened over time among a number of events and occurrences?

If it was a specific moment in time, pinpoint that moment in your mind. In fact, write it down.

If it was a number of moments over time, pinpoint those moments and write them down.

We'll call these "core memories". If you have ever watched Disney's *Inside Out*, then that will especially help you to visualize this with me. In the movie, the core memories are a major importance because they represent some of the main character, Riley's, major life events. They are more important than just normal memories because these memories have played a part in developing Riley's personality and who she is at present age. While it may not work quite exactly how Hollywood makes it appear, the reality is that we really do have key moments in our life that plays a part in molding who we are today.

With that being said, there are core memories that have played a part in causing you to lose the love you once had in leading. It's going to be important that you recognize those moments and call them to the forefront of your mind and write them down as I had mentioned. If you haven't already, take a moment to set this book down and start writing these moments before moving forward.

Part 2

HOW?

Next, we need to figure out how these core memories impacted

you. Obviously, it must have been in a negative way. So, think

back to those core memories. How did they cause you to feel

negative in those moments? Let me ask it in a different way: why

did you feel negative in those moments? What about it caused

you to feel negatively? Write your feelings down on the same

piece of paper. Be honest with yourself and just lay it all out.

These moments had a big impact on you, so it should be

important enough to be open with yourself about.

Use this as a guide to help you:

_____ made me feel _____ because
    (Core Memory)   (Emotion/How)

_____.
    (Why)

Again, take a moment to set this book down and start writing out how these moments made you feel and why you felt this way.

Now that you have identified what core moments caused your heart to change and we also know what it was about these moments that affected you in the way they did, we have to figure out what to do about it. The ultimate solution will vary far too much based on each situation, but allow me to ask a few questions to get your mind going. Think through these questions with an open heart.

1. Can it be reversed or altered to change the negative impact?
2. Should you talk to someone who can fix it? Who?
3. Did you respond appropriately?
4. Is it truly how you perceive it to be? Are you looking at the situation(s) at face value?
5. Have you prayed about it?
6. Have you discussed your feelings with someone else to gain their thoughts?

Part 2

7. Were others affected as well? How did they respond?

8. What needs to happen for you to move forward?

The answers to these questions will look completely different for every scenario, but I hope they will help you in determining the best route to take. Ultimately, finding the solution is up to you. And before you can ever try to move your organization forward, you have to move yourself forward. You can't lead your organization somewhere that you can't go or aren't willing to go, first. Once you find that peace and freedom from whatever it is that's been restraining you, you will be able to make a world of more difference in your organization as you lead! We've all been through a wilderness season where it felt like nothing but drought everywhere you turned, but the wilderness seasons are also where we grow the most!

Your heart being in proper alignment is so vital for the success of your organization. You need to make up in your mind and heart that you are going to do whatever it takes to get there. You've hopefully already done most of the hard work by writing it all down, now you just have to execute it. Do yourself a great favor and don't let this problem fester any longer. Remember from an earlier chapter, any problem that is allowed to remain will only continue to cause more problems and will be more difficult to resolve. There will always be repercussions because change is needed and they will only continue to grow as they are allowed to do so.

Allow me to leave you with one last story before we continue. At the time of me writing this chapter, my wife and I are in the process of building our first home. Earlier this week, we were able to do a final walk through of our home before going to closing. In this walk through, we

When things are allowed to go left unchecked, major things can go awry and even cause unhealthy environments for those around.

met with our Project Manager who gave us a ton of information regarding the care of our new home, warranty information, and all of that fancy legal stuff. We started on the main floor, went upstairs, and then finished in the basement. While we were in the basement, he pointed out a Radon Pass-Through Pipe. He stated that this pipe would be used to pull Radon from below the house and up through our roof, and would be especially important if we were to ever experience high levels of Radon. If our levels of Radon were ever to get to an unsafe level and not pulled out of our home, it could cause a number of issues, including cancer. While it's not required, it is wise to occasionally have these levels checked in our home, because if they do get high, it could cause an unsafe environment until it's fixed.

The reason I share this with you is because sometimes it's when things are allowed to go left unchecked that major things can go awry and even cause unhealthy environments for those around. As a leader, we have to start with ourselves and work our way out from there. If we let ourselves go unchecked, we'll never be able to get anything else in alignment. Often times, it's honestly and genuinely done out of complete innocence with no harm intended. Let this be our wake-up call to start being more intentional on doing more checkups more often!

Sometimes it's not that we are intentionally not being intentional, we are just being unintentional at being intentional. Read that again, and again until you get that. Leaders must be intentional!

I pray this chapter has helped you either to get back in alignment or solidify your confidence that you are in alignment and ready to tackle leading change in your organization. We have already come so far, but we still have so far that we need to go. I said this in the final paragraph of the last chapter, and I'll say it again: put a smile on your face, leader. You're making a difference in your own life and those around you! Now, are you ready to start finding a solution to your organization's problems? I really hope that you are. Let's go!

Part 2

Five

Dirty Work

My wife and I had just been put in as the new and first-ever Young Adult Pastors at our church when the Coronavirus infiltrated America and a lot of the world. We had been leading the YA Ministry for a solid three months when everything started shutting down. Our Pastor announced one Sunday that we would be cancelling all activities and going to only Sunday Morning worship until further notice in order to limit our time around each other. Before the next Sunday even came, we were online only indefinitely. There were a lot of different opinions and emotions from all angles, but we were all caught off guard to say the least. I think we can all agree that we never expected over a year to go by and we would still be wearing masks everywhere we went. Alas, that was our reality.

Being quarantined and not on campus for several months really caused us to get creative on how we would keep our core group together and pour into their lives until we were able to meet again in person. Luckily for us, my wife grew up in this church and I had already been around for a couple of years, so we both already knew the group pretty well. Regardless, we had never worried about keeping everyone together virtually before. We were so accustomed to having events, gatherings, and other means of being around each other that every time we came up with an incredibly brilliant idea we realized it involved being together in person. That was something we couldn't do at first.

Beyond that, the virus also caused us to really start thinking about how we can pour into our young adults in a more impactful way once we were able to meet in person again. We truly wanted to make a difference with this new ministry. One day, my wife and I sat down and developed an anonymous survey full of questions that would help us to understand where our young adults were spiritually and in what areas we needed to focus on growth. To give you an idea of what the questions were like, I've made a list of some of them. If you lead a similar ministry, I would recommend doing a survey like this as well to get a true grasp of where your group is spiritually.

1. How would you describe your walk with God?

2. How often do you set aside time for prayer?

3. How much time do you typically spend in prayer?

4. How would you describe your time in prayer? Do you feel that it is intentional and focused or without purpose and easily distracted?

5. How often do you set aside time in your day to read the Bible?

6. How much time do you typically spend reading the Bible?

7. How would you describe your time reading the Bible?

8. How often do you set aside at least a 24-hour period for fasting?

Part 2

9. What level of understanding do you feel that you have

    regarding your calling in life?

You may think I'm weird for this, but I honestly get giddy inside

just thinking about this again because of how much I love data

and statistics. Once Sarah and I sent this survey out to our young

adults to respond to the questions, we were so excited to start

seeing the responses come through. We really had a deep desire

to know where our young adults stood spiritually and to

understand how we could better serve them. We gave it a day or

two and eventually checked all of the responses that had come

in. We had a surprisingly great response rate and were beyond

pleased to see they had taken the time to do this for us. Which, I

suppose in reality they had nothing but time to do it since we

were all quarantined at home.

The results, though, weren't what we hoped they would be. I

wouldn't say that we were shocked necessarily, but deep down

you always hope for better. We quickly discovered that only a

small fraction of our young adults spent time reading the Word

of God on a regular basis or in prayer. None of them had a

routine of fasting. Their responses showed us that when they did decide to pray or read, it was for very short stints of time and they gained very little from it. Nearly none of them had any inclination as to what their purpose and calling in life was.

Naturally, these results devastated my wife and I. We had a great assignment set before us and we knew that we had to do what we could to help our young adults grow in their walk with Christ. We spent nearly an entire year researching studies, books, and curriculum that could potentially be used to help cover all of these bases for us. I would order a study that I thought would be helpful, only to realize that it simply wasn't it and be back to ground zero. It was a major struggle but was something we wouldn't give up on until we found what we were looking for - whatever that was. We knew our group well enough to know what they would and wouldn't connect with. At one point, I had even started looking into developing our own curriculum that we could use.

After nearly a year of research, I found myself talking one day to a youth pastor at a church in our denomination about forty-five minutes from ours who had just moved to the area from another

Part 2

state. My intention initially was only to introduce myself and welcome him to the area. As conversation continued, we eventually began talking about how our ministries are structured and what studies we have used in the past. After I briefly explained my dilemma, he recommended a particular study to me that had actually been written by another Pastor not far from us and told me where I could order the curriculum. I ordered the leader's guide to this study a few days later and upon receiving it in the mail and looking it over, I knew I had found what I was looking for! It took almost a year of research and a conversation with a Youth Pastor who had just moved to my area to get there, but I finally found it! I knew that this was the study that would be used to make an eternal difference in the young adults who were a part of our ministry.

Researching possible solutions can be exhaustive and take up way more time than you thought it would ever take you, but in the end it's absolutely worth it! Again, this is why you have to love your organization and be in alignment. When you are researching options to find a solution, you have to know your organization well enough to discern whether or not it will work in your context. You must research options that will align with the Core Values, Mission, and Vision. There will be moments where you even have to put your opinions to the side and look at it at face value and be totally bi-partisan.

Five Stages of Research

Depending on who you talk to, there are anywhere between five and nine stages of research. Ultimately, it's all the same but some formats will break it down into more stages or less. For our purpose, I'm going to go with the format that only uses five stages (you're welcome). It's important that you know these

stages and we talk about them a little bit because it's imperative that you 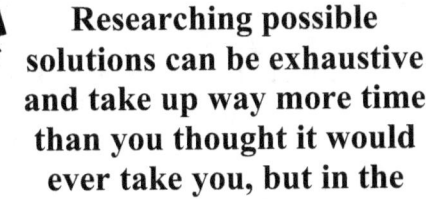 **Researching possible solutions can be exhaustive and take up way more time than you thought it would ever take you, but in the end it's absolutely worth it!**

follow these stages to reach an appropriate solution.

Think of these five stages as tools that you are placing inside your toolbox to help you build what you need. Without these tools, you will never be able to conduct and construct the research that needs to happen for a successful end. You may have other tools and ideas on how to get to the end, but if you try to complete construction using improper tools, you will likely discover your finished product is faulty and in need of repair before you even begin to use it. Let's take a look at these five very important and necessary stages of research.

1. Identify the Problem

Now this certainly sounds familiar, doesn't it? That's right, the very first step in the research process is identifying the problem. But guess what? We've already done that! Remember, you can't fix a problem you cannot see!

2. Designing the Research Project

This step will be easy for you to want to skip, but trust me you don't want to! Starting a research project blindly and without any organization will lead you down a path that will lead you virtually nowhere. Designing a research plan is the framework of how you will conduct your research and move forward with the project. Ultimately, you need to design a study that will test the hypotheses of interest, determine possible answers to the research questions, and provide the information needed for decision making. You need to determine what you think might be the solution to your problem and begin to put it to the test through your research. When Sarah and I sent out the study to our young adults, we later found out that they were not at all spiritually in the place we thought they were. This caused us to completely change how we were going to move forward with leading. Our original intentions were to start teaching on the Book of Revelation upon returning to campus, but we realized they weren't even reading their Bible or praying. Revelation was far too deep of a study for a group who rarely spent time reading Scripture. We needed to go back to the basics and work our way up, and that's exactly what we did!

3. Collect Data

This is where we really start digging into new ground. Once you've identified the problem, it's time to start doing some research to finding the solution that best fits your organization. Use resources that are available to you and are relevant to what you're looking for. For example, when I was looking for new curriculum or material to use for my young adult ministry, I didn't go to the Public Library and ask them to guide me to the Chemistry books! Instead, I started looking at websites that I was familiar with who carried solid and reputable discipleship material. I also decided to post on a few groups that I'm a part of on Facebook and other social media sites that are specifically for young adult ministry leaders. Through doing this, I was not only able to view untold numbers of pages worth of curriculum available, but I was also able to get input and insight from others to see what they have used in the past and what worked for them. Ultimately, this stage is all about seeing what other people are saying and what their insights have to offer.

4. Interpret Data

The stage of interpreting your data will help you truly get a grip on where you are at. For me, I realized a number of times that the possible solutions of discipleship material weren't at all what I was needing or looking for. I didn't even look at any of them as potential solutions. They were just straight up a "no", to be completely honest. That's okay. You just return back to stage three and keep looking. Ideally, though, you will find yourself with a couple of viable solutions that could work. Some will come with certain pros and cons and others will come with their own. They will match your organization's Core Values, Mission, and Vision, and are completely fair solutions that can just as easily work. At this point, you will want to begin organizing all of the information you gathered and make it easily readable to those who may be on the receiving end. You want to lay out all of the information before you and make it very clear to anyone who may be reading it. Most likely, you will be presenting the information to either a superior or a board that will also play a part in the decision making process. They need to be able to look at the information and be equally as knowledgeable about it as you are! We will talk about this one a little more in the next chapter.

5. Report

This is the last and final stage of research, and we will talk about this in a later chapter!

Part 2

Researching solutions for change is dirty work. Unless you're a freak of nature, like myself, then it probably doesn't entice you very much to spend hours and hours at a time in front of a computer screen, phone, or with books laid out in front of you while you try to figure out which route to take. While it's not fun, it will make the process much smoother and easier if you keep everything organized.

Activity

Let's do a similar activity like what we did in the last chapter and let's start writing all of these things out. Either get sheet of paper and make it to match my example below or use the space I've given to write in the book and help you as a guide. Go ahead and fill out steps 1-2 but stop there. We'll pick up with more on steps 3-4 in the next chapter.

RESEARCH

1. Identify the Problem

What is the problem you are experiencing?

_____

_____

2. Design the Research Project

What do you think are potential solutions?

_____

_____

_____

What is your plan of action to research whether these solutions

will or won't work?

_____

_____

_____

3. Collect Data

Proceed with your research.

4. Interpret Data

What were your findings? Were the potential solutions found to

still be viable or not? Were other potential solutions discovered?

Part 2

_____

_____

_____

5. Report

Clean up your findings and prepare them to be presented.

Five Research Tips

Let me give you some quick research tips that you may also want to keep in mind as you are researching options. I would most definitely be wrong to make you think I have it all figured out, but I believe these tips will help you as you are researching. These tips aren't necessarily "Gospel truth" that must be followed, but you will find your research to be much more successful if you will use them as a guide in how you search for solutions.

1. Start big, then hone into specifics

Sometimes you may realize that you don't know what the solution may potentially be to the problem(s) you have identified. It may be smart to start your search to be general and then hone into specifics as you begin to get a better understanding of what you're looking for. Online resources like Google or any other search engine will be a good way to start off and then work from there. While you need to realize the results aren't always the most accurate, it will get you started on some key points or lead you to articles of what others have said.

2. Recognize a quality source

Learning how to recognize what a quality source is will be huge for you. Over the years, I have found solutions that I even engaged with thinking that it was a really good solution, only to later realize that it honestly wasn't and there should have been some obvious red flags raised. For example, one time I was on the phone with a customer support agent for a particular software that my church was using. We kept getting an error code and couldn't figure out what the issue was, so I gave them a call for further technical support. While I was on the phone with this support agent, she told me that the only resource she had to go off of was Google. There was no internal technical support database for her to reference. To say that I was appalled and beyond amazed at this would be an understatement! How could a company rely on what other's said on Google for solutions to their products' own technical problems?! Ladies and gentlemen, this was not a quality product! As you are researching options, you really want to dive deep into what kind of source is providing the feedback that is being given. How reputable are they? Are they well known? What credentials do they have to offer? These are all very important questions that you need to consider and ask yourself as you come across articles and websites offering their thoughts, opinions, and advice!

Jesus said in Matthew 7:20 (NKJV), "Therefore you will know them by their fruits." In other words, you will be able to tell whether or not there is legitimacy based on what kind of products are being produced. I have made a decision to go with one solution versus another at times simply because I knew that a number of well-known and credible ministries also used the same solution. The product was showing fruit because of how many others whom I looked up to were satisfied with their results of using it. When researching for solutions, I go to organizations who are at a level that I aspire to be for advice. Not to speak ill of organizations that are smaller, but I'm always looking to level up. Would you ever go to an organization smaller than yours and ask for advice on how you can grow? Of course not! That doesn't mean that a smaller organization is any less significant, but it makes the most sense to go to an organization larger to gain insight on growth. Learn to recognize what a quality source is in your searching!

3. Verify information

Depending on what you are researching, you may find dozens or even hundreds of website results that will give you answers for what you are looking for. Anytime you are being given any kind of information that can be fact checked, you want to be sure that you do! If a website claims that the product has a one-year warranty, double check the information by some other means to confirm whether this is true and what that warranty entails. For the most part, people can say pretty much whatever they want to online, so don't take anything for granted.

Part 2

Paul wrote that "every matter must be established by two or three witnesses" (2 Corinthians 13:1 NIV) when he was writing to the Corinthian church. This was the legal requirement for accepting any evidence at trial in the church. Paul wanted to be sure that any information he was accepting to be true could first stand witness among multiple people. This tells me that verifying information and double and triple checking it to be true is very important to God - and should be to us as well!

4. Keep an open mind

You may quickly realize that the results you are finding aren't exactly what you originally thought they would be. This doesn't mean that the results must be wrong, it may mean that you just need to keep an open mind to go in a different direction than what you had intended to go. Good research is meant to find good answers - not necessarily solidify your preconceived notions. If you are merely researching to solidify what you think you already know, you will be forced to omit legitimate findings solely because they don't match.

5.   Stay organized

If you're like me, you are a firm believer in organization and everything being orderly and having its rightful place. If you're not like me, you probably struggle a little bit more in this field. It's not that you're a bad person - it's okay to be wrong sometimes (kidding!). In all seriousness, staying organized with your information will be a saving grace. Especially if you begin collecting a lot of information on a number of possible solutions, it's important to keep everything organized so that information doesn't get mismatched and associated with the wrong thing. Figure out what kind of organization system works best for you and stick to it! Paul told the Corinthian Church, "but all things should be done decently and in order" (1 Corinthians 14:40 ESV). Once again, we see a principle that appears to be very important to God and should be important to us as well! It's not a bad thing to be organized. In fact, it's a very good thing and is even more important for any leader.

I promise that you want to keep these tips in mind as you move forward with the researching process. Write them down if you need to or highlight them in the book. Do whatever you need to in order to keep them in the forefront of your mind. Being a catalyst for change is a great responsibility and you are being left with making a difference in your organization or whatever context may apply to you. After reading this chapter, you should be in a good place to start researching ideas. This stage in the process is going to look so different for every single individual. Regardless, though, the process and tips all stay the same. Sure, you may have to look at it from a different angle, but that's okay! Again, this book can be made relevant to absolutely any situation, any leader, any organization, any business, any family, and any individual. It's only irrelevant if you want to make it out to be!

As you proceed forward and begin your research process, be sure to follow these steps:

1. Start big, then hone into specifics

2. Learn to recognize what a quality source looks like. Look to those whom you admire and aspire to be like!

3. Verify information among two or three sources

4. Keen an open mind and realize the results you're getting may not look like what you thought they would

5. Stay organized

It's time to start digging into the dirty work, my friend. You were made for this and you are making a difference in the lives of those around you. I will be the first to admit and realize that this probably isn't the most exciting and exhilarating chapter that this book or the world has to offer. But, it's packed full of practical advice and steps on how you can perform effective research that will help you get results that you're looking for and need to move your organization forward. You can spend hours, days, weeks, months, and years attempting to find answers and completely miss them or settle for something less simply because you didn't have the right tools in your toolbox. Get to researching and then let's keep moving forward!

Part 2

Six

Don't Make a Decision

Yep, you read those words above correctly. Don't make a decision. Not really what you were expecting, huh? Trust me, this isn't a hook line to try and get you drawn in only to read the chapter and make it more interesting. I'm actually being 100% honest with you on this.

If you are reading these words, hopefully that means you have done all of your research, found some possible solutions, and are now ready for decision-making time. Don't put the cart before the horse, though. There's still some things that we need to talk through and think through before you proceed any further. At this point, it's very important to really understand what your role is and what the expectations of your role are. Unfortunately, there have been well-meaning leaders who have been given projects in their organization and knocked it out of the park - until they stepped out of their lane and went beyond the scope of authority that was originally intended for them by their superior. One of the most difficult situations to be in is trying to handle an individual who assumes more authority than what has actually been given.

If you are not the individual who has the say in making a final decision, then be very careful not to do that very thing. Here's what I mean - as you are researching and finding potential solutions to the problem that is at stake, you are naturally going to find a number of possibilities that all seem like good and even great ideas. Your role in the project is to find probably two or three really solid options and present them to your leader. Your job is *not* to make the decision for the leader and decide for yourself that one particular solution is the one that should be instituted. While you certainly have the right to own your opinion and perhaps even express it to your leader, it is the leader who should ultimately decide which route is the best to take. After all, that is what the leader has been placed in their position to do.

Honest Mistakes

My wife and I were recently at Sam's Club getting a few groceries after church on a Sunday before we headed home to fix lunch. We were walking down the main aisle when we decided that we would split up and Sarah would go over to Produce to pick up what we needed there, while I would go to the very back and get a pack of water bottles. As she turns and goes toward Produce, I continue walking straight to the back wall full of water bottles. I found the brand we like to get, put it in the bottom of the cart, and head toward the produce to find my wife. We pick up a few other items, check out, and head toward the car to load our groceries in the back and head home. As we are unloading our groceries, we get everything in the back of the car except for the water bottles in the bottom of the cart when

Part 2

suddenly it hits my wife and I like a ton of bricks. We forgot to scan and pay for the water at Self-Checkout! Sarah looks at me and says, "We'll have to go back inside and pay for it," as I'm looking at her in dread knowing that I am the one that will have to deal with it and was not in the mood to do so whatsoever. Nonetheless, we have to do the right thing. I tell Sarah to go ahead and get in the car and I would run back inside and pay for the water really quick. We eventually make it home at last and bring everything inside. As we are beginning to put our groceries away, I realize as I'm ripping the plastic off of the water bottle packaging to load the bottles in the refrigerator that I managed to get the wrong ones! *You've got to be kidding me.* After all of the trouble these stupid water bottles have caused me, and I didn't even get the right ones. We typically always prefer to get the 20oz water bottles, but I had accidentally picked up the 16.9oz bottles. Sure, it's extremely minute and sounds stupid and petty (and probably is), but in the moment it was beyond aggravating. Both of the things that happened with the water - not paying for it originally and picking up the wrong ones - were both very much unintentional and honest mistakes. And even though it was extremely aggravating, you want to know the reality of both of those mistakes? They were both easily resolved and don't really matter. When I realized that we didn't pay for the water, I simply went back in and payed for it. When I realized I picked up the wrong size bottles, we just drank them anyways. Neither of these mistakes had any significant bearing on our lives. These things happen every single day.

Here's an incredible truth you greatly need to realize - when the stakes are a whole lot higher than picking out the wrong water bottles for your refrigerator at home, don't put yourself in a place of making major and altering decisions if you're not supposed to.

Honest mistakes made outside of permissible authority aren't honest at all - they're just mistakes.

And they could be extremely costly to you, those around you, and your organization. Please hear me out and see my heart. If you aren't sure what the expectations are for you, don't be afraid to ask for clarification. Saying you didn't know rarely comes with reasonable excuse. When driving on the highway, it's your responsibility to know what lane you're driving in, where the lane markings are, and when your lane ends. Likewise, it's your responsibility to know the same in leadership and when working under a superior. And even a superior has other superiors they must answer to. There is also an allowed scope of authority.

Biases

Besides not wanting to step beyond your scope of authority, here is another major reason that you want to refrain from making a decision on your own and only presenting one option to your leader: bias. No matter how great of a leader or person we may be, we all have this wonderful gift of bias. When we have a bias against

 **Honest mistakes made outside of permissible authority aren't honest at all - they're just mistakes.**

something, it means we have an unfair prejudice or thought pattern about or toward a person, thing, or idea. Usually based off previous personal experience, we have a preconceived notion that implants certain feelings to rise up within us regarding these things. It's like a flash back to a particular moment in time every time we think about it.

As someone who is researching ideas and solutions for your organization, you are naturally going to let bias play some part in the research process. It's inevitable as unfair as it may be. In all reality, some bias is okay. The truth of the matter is that bias isn't necessarily unreasonable. There's likely good reasoning behind your bias. Still yet, there must come a point where the bias has to end - and once you've narrowed your options down to two or three is precisely where that end must come.

Here's why - there are likely to be biases that you have, perhaps that you don't even realize about yourself, that would cause you to cancel a solution out as an option. Meanwhile, your leader doesn't share that same bias and it would have never played a part in their final decision making process. You need some help with examples of what I'm trying to lay down? I'm glad you asked! Take a look at some of these potential biases:

- Too cheap or too expensive

- Too easy or too difficult

- Not impactful enough or too impactful

- Takes too long or doesn't take long enough

- Will be received well or won't be received well

- Not enough credibility or plenty of credibility

The list could go on and on for pages, but I think you get the idea. While you are thinking that a particular solution may be entirely too expensive, it could actually be totally worth it and perhaps even in the right wheelhouse that your leader was thinking would be spent! Don't try to make the decision for the leader and determine for yourself that something is too expensive or will be too difficult, etc. Let the leader make that decision! Understanding this is extremely important and is why I placed this chapter before presenting the information to the leader, if that person isn't you.

Narrowing Down

Now you should be ready to start narrowing down some of the options that you found. As I said before, I would recommend bringing two to three options to present to your leader. Unless, of course, they have instructed otherwise. Generally speaking, I personally believe this is not only the proper way to handle it, but is also showing your leader that you are submitting to their complete control and authority to make the final decision.

I have said this probably a hundred times already and I'm going to say it at least once more - when finding a solution, it absolutely must line up with your organization's core values, mission, and vision. This is a non-negotiable. You can automatically start marking out any solutions that could possibly jeopardize any of these principles. Next, start evaluating the solutions that appear to be a negative outlier - these are solutions that you may have come across that perhaps match your organization's principles, but it is very obvious and apparent that solution simply wouldn't work for a number of possible reasons. In this instance, you may be displaying some bias, but it's likely using common sense far more than it is bias. You know your organization well and you know what solution "just isn't it". Once you've done this and still have more than two or three solutions, start evaluating the remaining solutions at face value

Part 2

and rank your top three choices - unless your leader has requested more or less, and assuming that at least three options still remain. Again, these solutions should not be selected out of bias (see the earlier list for a reminder). Allow your organization's principles and your own common sense lead you to your final list of solutions. I realize this probably sounds entirely too simple, but if you try it you might just be surprised! Trust that gut instinct of yours. You are a leader. This is what you do!

This has been more of a subchapter in length, but I felt it extremely necessary to throw this in and offer some additional guidance and direction before moving forward. You have already come an incredible way in being a catalyst for change and remember - you are making a difference! What you are doing matters. Thank you for leading with integrity and being a leader with courage. I hope you will take the time to go over the Part 2 Discussion Questions to keep your mind going in the right direction as we move forward to Part 3. Let's keep it moving!

PART TWO

DISCUSSION

QUESTIONS

1. Would you consider yourself in or out of alignment with your organization? Why?

2. What core memories play a role in how you feel about your organization?

3. What struggles did you experience during research?

Part 2

4. What did you enjoy about research?

5. Do you feel that you have a deep certainty about your scope of authority assigned to you? Why or why not?

6. Do you find it easy or difficult to ignore certain biases during research? Why?

7. What options did you remove as possibilities? Why?

Part 3

Engage with Change

Part 3

Seven

The Presentation

If there is any chapter within the covers of this book that you

are going to be most likely to either completely skip or merely

skim through, it's probably going to be this one.

Wait, can I actually say that? Oh well.

It really is true, though. This is an extremely practical book with

a lot of very practical teaching and advise. This chapter is meant

to be a guide that will help walk you through the process of preparing for the actual presentation of the solutions you have found. No, this isn't a boring college textbook that you're required to read in some Ed.D course. But details do matter. A lot, actually. Even if you think that the presentation is what you have down the best and are most experienced in, read this chapter anyways. Some of you won't even be giving a presentation, you'll only be having a talk with a family member or close friend. I totally get it. Read this chapter anyways.

Proverbs 12:15 says, *"The way of a fool is right in his own eyes, But he who heeds council is wise."*(NKJV)

In other words, you are a fool to think that your own way is always the right way. A wise person will listen to the advice of others. As harsh as that may seem, it's completely true. There is a reason that some people never grow, get better, or level up in life and it's often because they are too stubborn to heed council from someone else. They have in their mind what is right and only that will they follow. I would beg you not to be a foolish person as you read my words, but a wise person. Please be rest assured I don't claim to know anywhere near as much as others

may. Notice the Proverb doesn't say anything about the council

being wise or good, only the matter of fact that to heed (or listen)

to council is wise. You may get to the end of this chapter and

realize that everything I said is complete garbage and is of no

use. If that happens, I still accomplished my goal because I

helped you solidify your beliefs on how a presentation should

flow. If you finish reading this chapter and you gained insight

and thoughts you haven't had before, then I accomplished my

goal yet again! Shall we get started?

Where Do You Land?

I really don't remember a ton about my Elementary School days,

but I certainly remember enough about Middle School and High

School to still feel

that terrible gut

feeling I had every

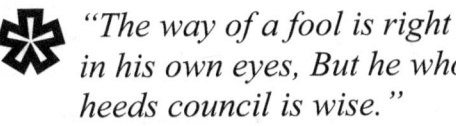

"The way of a fool is right in his own eyes, But he who heeds council is wise."
- Proverbs 12:15

time I knew that we

were doing a presentation in class. You would think that since I

had started preaching at the age of 16 that I wasn't one who didn't enjoy getting up in front of people, but I regress. For whatever reason, there was just something about doing a presentation at school that I hated.

Naturally, most of us are that way and is actually one of the top fears that people have, according to several studies. I am a true introvert, I'll admit, but I have grown out of my shell tremendously over the years. When I was younger, there was no doubt about Zach Prewitt being a shy kid. I knew it, my parents knew it, kids at school knew it, the mailman knew it. Okay, maybe the mailman didn't know. Or did he? Probably. Either way, you get the idea. I was extremely shy. It honestly took me even beyond High School and College before I ever truly starting coming out of my shell. Over the years, that terrible gut feeling before getting in front of people has changed big time and I actually enjoy getting up in front of people - whether it be to preach, teach, train, or present information. I thank God for that change in me, because otherwise being a Pastor would be miserable! The point being - if you hate getting in front of people to talk, I understand you completely.

The Presentation

I'm not really sure where exactly you fall in terms of hating presentations or loving it. Statistically, you're probably leaning more toward hating it. Obviously this is going to play a great bearing on whether you are looking forward to presenting your findings to your superior or if you would prefer an easier and less painful route such as having a toenail ripped off instead. I imagine that since you are a leader and play an important role in your organization, you probably have at least some level of comfort in presenting, despite enjoying it or not. Hopefully this is the case for you, anyways.

Nonetheless, this is the place that we find ourselves. You have done all of the dirty work and have made it an incredible distance in recognizing the need for change and finding a list of possible solutions to the problem at hand. Now, it's time to get ready for a presentation to your superior and/or board. In this chapter, I'm going to lead you through the entire process from gathering your information together to present all the way to the end presentation. It's important to remember that I can only provide you with a guide that will help lead you through this process to ensure you are creating an effective presentation that will properly highlight what you have worked so hard on. Based on your organization and what your context is, everything I say may not be applicable. As a leader, it's important to be able to recognize what will meet the standards of your superior and organization.

Pre - Presentation

Everything you do leading up to the presentation is equally as important, if not more important, than the presentation itself. Here is a very simple yet important equation to remember:

Great information + Great communication = successful presentation

If there is not both great information and great communication, you cannot have a successful presentation. You can speak in the most eloquent manner and engage with your audience like a pro, but if you don't have full and complete details about what you are presenting, then your presentation is of little to no value to those listening. Likewise, you can have incredible information that is complete, thought out, and well organized, but if you are

consistently distracted, can't complete your thoughts, and have a

terrible time with eye contact and engaging your audience, they

will likely be zoned out and little interested in what you have to

say. In both cases, you weren't able to accomplish the goal of

your presentation. This is why it's important to follow these

steps before your presentation so that you can prepare to give a

proper presentation that will be meaningful, impactful, and

engaging.

1. Gather all information

The first step you need to take in your pre-presentation phase is

to gather all of the information that you have found on your two-

to-three solutions. You want to be sure that you know what

you're talking about.
Think about all
possible information
that may be needed

If there is not both great information and great communication, you cannot have a successful presentation.

and make sure you have it available. While it may not be

possible to foresee everything, you want to avoid missing any details that could cause a potential unseen problem later that could have easily been avoided. You want to be able to give your superior a crystal clear picture of what possible solutions you are giving them so they can make an appropriate decision. You don't want any details, especially important ones, left out. You should know what that looks like based on your circumstance and context.

2. Organize

Organization is probably one of my top priorities in everything I do. If something is unorganized, it irks me to no end and causes my focus to be directed toward the mess more than anything else. Not only do you not want your superior to see that you are an unorganized individual, but you also don't want them to be distracted and unable to focus on the presentation of what you are giving them. Organization is a huge key to your success as a leader. Take the time to read through all of your information and clean it up to make it clear, easy to follow, and reader friendly. Ensure the information is staged in an order that makes the most sense. The presentation should start at a very basic level and the information will begin to build upon another.

Since you have more than one solution at hand, it may serve you well to prepare a comparison sheet that compares and contrasts the major points of each solution. This will help you and others to quickly see how the solutions compare to each other. It may be decided that a con automatically removes a solution as being top choice or a pro automatically improves a solution as being a possible top choice. Being able to see the solutions side-by-side will be a great tool to provide at the end of your presentation.

3. Supporting Documents

Next, you want to ensure that you have all necessary supporting documents. This could be statistics, reviews, formal papers, journal entries, or anything else that may have played an integral part of your research process and caused you to select a particular solution as being a top three option. While you may determine that certain pieces of supporting documents are appropriate for the official presentation, these will most likely only be used as a talking point or to be provided upon being asked. If you wish, you can always provide this information in print form to your superior for them to review if they wish, but not something you spend time on as you are presenting. What's most important is that you at least have the information at hand and can provide support for your findings.

4. Presentation Design

Now you are really getting ready to wrap this thing up to present! You want to determine what your presentation should look like. Do you want a PowerPoint? Do you want a packet of information to hand out? Do you want both? Do you want graphics or videos? These all need to be

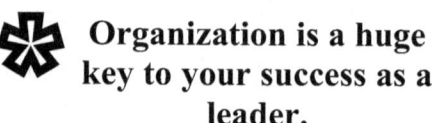

Organization is a huge key to your success as a leader.

considered and determined what is most appropriate for your context and what will be most effective for presenting. Once you figure out what that is, get to designing and putting your presentation material together! If you need helping designing, Microsoft Office has great template options and others can be found on the internet to download as well. Double check for spelling and any other errors that may be present. You may even want to consider having someone else who is able to be privy of the information to double check your work and give honest opinions as well. At this point, all of the hard work has been done. Now, you are just moving the information into a format that is most conducive for your context to present it.

5. Prepare for Questions

This part can be tricky because it's impossible to know the answer to every single question that could be asked. What's important is that you know as much information about your solutions as possible so that you are well equipped to answer virtually anything about it.

In one sense you're like a salesman. You are trying your best to sell something. In another sense, you're the opposite of a salesman, because you have to be up front and open about all the good and the bad, too. A salesman knows every small and intricate detail about what they are selling because they have to know what could win them a sale or what could potentially cost them a sale. They are ready for it all. You need to be equally prepared to be hit from all angles and know what you are talking about as much as possible. It's almost as if you are operating in a SME (Subject Matter Expert) role at this point. You're expected to know a whole lot about all solutions you are presenting.

6. Study

The work has been done and you have done everything you can to form the presentation in the best possible manner. Now, it's time to study. You want to go through your notes time and time again until you have it memorized and are well versed in all of the points you are making. The less time you spend looking at your notes and the more time you are able to focus on engaging with your audience, the better. Being able to go through your presentation with fewer notes will help your superior know that you have done your research and you know what you are talking about, which will increase their confidence in what you are giving them. They will know you can be trusted and that you took this project seriously enough to come prepared.

You have been entrusted with a very important task as a leader. Whether you are leading major or minor change, whether it impacts a small department or even your own family, or if it impacts a very large organization and a lot of lives, what you are doing matters! If you haven't yet realized that, here is your reality check. It is a selfish thought to think that your actions won't affect anyone else. Your actions never only affect you. They will always affect someone else as well. You have been entrusted to play an important part in leading change and it will have an impact. The size of impact is completely irrelevant. It should never be taken lightly.

Presentation

You have a great responsibility as a leader and now it's time to walk in it and show your superior what changes are being made available to the organization. You need to be able to give the presentation in a way that honors their time and to be ready to lay out all of the details in an organized manner.

Part 3

1. Plan to Prepare

One of the first things you need to do before the day of the presentation is determine the details of the meeting - date, time, place, who will be in attendance, etc. The reason being is because you will want to plan to arrive early, if possible, to prepare so that you are able to begin presenting at the scheduled time. Again, honoring your superior's time should be a priority. This isn't to mean that you should feel rushed. There is a difference! By making sure that you have your presentation up and ready to begin is honoring their time. This also allows you time if something doesn't go as planned or if you have technology issues. Being prepared and ready to go will take a huge burden off your shoulder as you are getting ready to present.

2. Welcome

As you are beginning your presentation, make a special point to greet your superior or anyone else sitting under the presentation, and thank them for their time. You should remember that they have taken this concern upon themselves enough to take time out in order to listen to what solutions you have found and to do what it takes to provide better for the organization and those impacted.

3. Summarize

Take a few moments to summarize why they are even there in the first place. Be clear on what the problem is that you are attempting to solve and increase their understanding on what repercussions are being experienced within the organization because of the problem at hand. This will help ensure they are on the same page with you regarding the significance of finding a resolve. If you can't first get them to agree there is a problem, they will never have any need to determine a solution!

4. Solutions

Next, you will have the opportunity to present your possible solutions and all of the most important details regarding them. This is where it's important to take your time, be sure that you are being clear, and engage with your superior and those listening. It's your job to make sure they are getting every single piece to the puzzle. If it's a 100-piece puzzle, you have to make sure you're giving them all 100 pieces and to show how they all come together. I have found myself giving a presentation or teaching before and you think that you have communicated clearly and everything you are saying is being grasped by those listening, only to be talking to one of them later and realize they only picked up about 10 of the 100 pieces you were laying down. Not only is that extremely frustrating because it was a complete waste of time, but you also spent all of that effort and time only for them to completely miss the information you were trying to convey! This is why your preparation beforehand plays such an important role in the success of your presentation.

5. Conclusion

This is a great opportunity to bring out a Comparison Sheet that compares all of the pros and cons of each solution, if you created one. This will give your superior a final opportunity to review all of the information that you have given in a more tangible format. Use this time to wrap up and conclude any final thoughts that you may want to share.

6. Questions

Open the floor for discussion or for any questions that your superior or anyone else in the room may have regarding anything you have presented. This is most likely where your in-depth knowledge of the subject matter is going to come into great play.

If you follow each of those tips along with having great communication and great information, you will undoubtedly have given a successful presentation of solutions. We're not quite finished yet, though! I recommend at least completing the next chapter before you actually give your presentation. If possible, I would prefer you to have the entire book finished, but at least be sure to complete the next chapter so that you don't miss out on some important tips and advice!

Part 3

Eight

The Outcome

During my tenure on the Church & Pastor's Council at a
church I served at in my beginning years of ministry, we decided
to look at replacing our church sign that stood by the road. The
church was located near Downtown of a smaller-to-mid-sized
city and had quite a bit of road traffic passing by every single
day. At that point, we had been in our new building for about ten
years and there had been a lot of new technology and upgrades in
the sign industry since we had erected our new sign a decade
earlier. And by all of that, I mean to say that the church down the
road had one of those new red LED marquee signs, and we

weren't about to get showed up. Or at least that was going on in the back of my mind, anyways.

So, the council asked me if I could take this project on and gather some quotes and design options to bring back for the next meeting. Eager and excited to take on my first assignment, I gladly accepted. A few days later, I was able to figure out who we had purchased our current sign from and got in contact with one of the salesmen to see what options were available. I gave him some of the basic information of what we were looking for and asked if he could get us a couple of designs and quotes.

I also had an idea for a sign that came to my mind, so I drew it out the best I could on a piece of paper and sent it to the rep to design. I was beyond excited to see this one and just knew the council would love it! It was an absolutely stunning sign with a full color LED marquee (much better than the church down the street that could only do red), and on top was a world globe with the church logo in the middle. I went back and forth with the sales rep a number of times trying to work out the details to make sure this particular sign was exactly how I had imagined it.

I must confess, I spent far more time getting this sign to perfection than I did any of the other options he provided.

Man oh man, this was about to be the nicest church sign in the whole city! No doubt, this would be a sign that had other churches talking.

The day of our next council meeting finally arrives and I come prepared with all of the documents in hand and ready to show the council what brilliance I had come up with. I made sure that I used full color in copying these bad boys because I knew that once the council saw the sign I had designed, they would all be gawking and ready to tell me to call the rep and hit "GO!".

The meeting begins and we work our way through the agenda until we finally get to my slot to speak. I begin dispersing the packets of information for all three sign options I had gathered from the company, including my design idea, and went over all the details of each one. I left the best for last and never mentioned to anyone that I was the brains behind the one sign. I was just going to wait for the opportune moment to mention it once they started talking about how nice of a sign it was. Well, that's what I expected would happen, anyways, and expecting it rightfully so. I mean, how could anyone not love this sign?! So, I finish my presentation of all the options and the council begins discussing each one, asks a few questions, and has a lot of back and forth talk. I knew they all loved the sign I had created, but was waiting for the discussion to really spark and narrow down onto my sign.

Before I realize we've even had a decent amount of time to talk about all of the incredible signs I brought to the table, the discussion had ended and the final conclusion of the council was that a new sign just wasn't in the budget at the moment and it would be best to leave our current sign as it was. The meeting was adjourned and the discussion never went any further.

WHAT?! Are you kidding me?! Clearly no one realizes how much time I spent contacting the sign company and emailing back and forth for weeks on end to make sure that we had these designs to look at! I even took it upon myself to create a sign and have it designed, knowing that it would look incredible and was like no other church sign I had ever seen before. All of the hard work and effort seemed completely wasted. Granted, I never let a single soul know how disappointed I was. But I most definitely was.

As frustrating as it might be, there will absolutely be times where you have invested your resources and put a lot of hard work into researching solutions only to present it to your superior and it get rejected. In fact, there's no doubt you've put your creative juices to the work and thought it through to the fullest extent and tried your best to make it work. It will probably even seem unfair that you invested so much only to get absolutely no return. As frustrating as it may be, "*to obey is greater than sacrifice*" (1 Sam. 15:22 ESV). While your sacrifice requires much of you (which is why it's called a sacrifice), your obedience to serving your leader and your organization is far greater. Even if your sacrifice brings little to no reward, obedience always will!

My friend, Josiah Kennealy, once gave me this advice: *No* doesn't actually mean *no*. It just means *not here* or *not now*. But, be just as gracious to *no* as you are *yes*!

When a leader is telling you *no*, it most likely is not a *no* that will continue to be *no* forever and in all circumstances.

Think about it. Most of the time, it really means that now is just not a good time or it doesn't work in this particular context. At a different place and/or a different time, it may be *yes*. Regardless, we must learn to be just as gracious in their *no* as we are their *yes*. In fact, how you react and move forward in their *no* will show them far more about your character and ability to lead than how you react and move forward in their *yes* Your attitude in the *no* could determine your future *yes*.

Clear as Mud

Once a decision has been made, you need to be clear and understand fully what that decision is. If your proposal was rejected, begin thinking outside the box. Are there other ways you can proceed with change, with your leader's permission, that

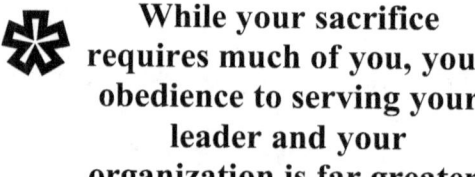 **While your sacrifice requires much of you, your obedience to serving your leader and your organization is far greater.** will at least help or alleviate the problem? Your best bet is to decipher

and understand what concerns your leader has that caused them to reject the proposed solutions. There is obviously something that must have turned them away from wanting to move forward. Have a conversation to determine what that is and ask your leader if they would be willing to have another conversation if you were able to find a solution that resolved that concern. Even if it isn't the preferred solution, but it at least helps with the problem to some degree.

    With my church sign assignment, I never thought about this at the time, but an excellent recommendation would have been to simply give our current sign a facelift. It would have been a much less expensive undertaking, but would have also allowed us to give the sign a fresh new look! I could have never been for sure that a facelift would have been approved, but since money was the primary concern, perhaps a facelift would have been a solution that would have fit the budget and been approved. You never know until you ask! Here is the reality of the matter - you and your leader both want what is best. You both want to see the organization operating at its fullest and best potential. Unless you have a leader who is completely unreasonable and doesn't actually want what's best, they will want to make a difference just as much, and more, as you do.

Part 3

Before you leave the meeting and walk away, you need to know what decision has been made and what your leader is thinking. Make sure that you and your leader are both on the same page. You don't want to leave that meeting with an unclear understanding of where everything stands. Understand this: Nothing is ever clear in a confused state. Take a moment and read that again. Truly process what I just said.

Nothing is ever clear in a confused state.

That statement is so basic that it's complex. But it's so powerfully true. If you leave your meeting in a confused state, unsure of what happened, what was decided, and where you're headed next, nothing will be clear to you. You will only leave with questions and no answers, and you will never be able to progress or move anything forward if you're not clear of where you're going. Don't leave in a confused state. Know where you stand and make sure everyone is leaving on the same page.

Next Steps

Once you know where you stand and where you're going, you can determine what your next steps are. Most likely, your next steps involve finding an alternative solution or moving forward with a solution you proposed. In my story with the church sign, there was nothing to move forward with because I didn't propose an alternative solution that would have solved both the problem at hand

Nothing is ever clear in a confused state.

(needing a new sign) and the budget concern. Don't be like me and miss this incredible opportunity! At the end of the day once all has been said and done, you may not have any next steps to move forward with. You may realize that you have hit the end of the road until a later time. But, if your proposed solutions have all been rejected, don't miss the opportunity to try to find a solution that may still work. If I would have thought to make the suggestion of giving our current sign a facelift, it very easily could have completely changed the end result. Instead, I accepted defeat without offering another way out where everyone wins. This isn't always avoidable, but don't be afraid to expend all ideas and thoughts.

What do your next steps look like? If you are like me with the church sign, my next steps should have been finding other solutions that may have worked. If nothing else, it never hurts to do a little bit of research to know what you're truly dealing with. In almost all situations, there is a solution that can work regardless of the restrictions and boundaries. It's only a matter of finding it. A true leader leads. A lot of times, that means making a way where there seems to be none. Again, the way out is there, you just have to find it. I wish I could go back and tell my 17-year-old self a few things and not to be so quick to sit down.

It's such an incredibly minor scenario, but I wonder how many of us have accepted an answer that we didn't like too quickly? I realize this may not be you in this particular situation, but truly think about that for a moment with me. How many times have you given up too quickly when you knew there had to be more that you could do? For some reason, you just quit. You gave up. You didn't pursue it any further. Here's the reality -

there are people out there, and within your organization, that are dying to see something come to fruition that you're too afraid to do anything about. You're not the only one that sees this hovering problem and wants something to be done about it, but no one has the courage to push the issue until something happens. So many of us accept things to be the way they are simply because someone else tells us that's how it is. Now let me clear: you should never rise up in retaliation or rebellion against your leader. This isn't wise nor is this what God would ever have you to do.

What I'm saying is that there will be times your leader says no simply because they don't see a solution that works. So, instead of accepting that as *no, period*, take that at it's true face value and realize that they are only saying *no* because you haven't found the right solution yet. It's your job to keep looking until you find that right solution. So here is what I'm really trying to get into your brain and heart here: even if you don't think there are any next steps, take them anyways. Keep pressing this thing forward and do what it takes. Don't go behind anyone's back or go beyond your scope of authority - just be a leader and lead. Quite frankly: do your job. This is what you're here for. If the answer is still *no* and it's a final *no with no exceptions*, then that's okay. But until you get a *no with no exceptions*, keep working until you find a *yes*. Don't sit down and quit like I did. No matter how

 There are people out there, and within your organization, that are dying to see something come to fruition that you're too afraid to do anything about.

big or small it may be, you'll end up reflecting over it years down the road and regret you didn't do more. Trust me.

If you are on the flip side of what I've been talking about so far, and you got a *yes* - Congratulations! This is exactly the moment you have worked so hard to get to and now it's beginning to pay off. At this point, you need to start looking at next steps and what the plan looks like moving forward with transitioning and implementation of the change. We will begin discussing this in the upcoming chapters.

Reflection

Before we move any further, though, I want to encourage you to take the time and reflect. At this point, you have poured so much into this project and have done countless hours of researching, prep work, and finally a presentation on everything you have gathered. Whether you got a *yes* or a *no*, this is still for you. Now that you have presented the solutions to your leader, take the time and reflect on everything you have done so far - the great, the good, the bad, and even the ugly. What would you change? What would you do differently next time? What needs to be adjusted moving forward as you work toward engaging with change? Here's why I'm having you do this: I think we overlook how important and impactful taking time to reflect can truly be. Now that you are at a crossroads and in-between phases of leading change, you have the perfect opportunity to do a reset. Whether you are going back to the drawing board or moving forward with an approved change, you have the chance to do better at what you were once doing okay or maybe even not so great at. There was no doubt some things that you handled or went about that you later realized wasn't the best or most

Part 3

effective way. Now is your time to make sure you go about it differently as you move into a new phase. Take the time to reflect and determine how you want to handle the project moving forward. Once you've done that, let's keep moving along!

Nine

Conflicting Change

Leading change is great and all - until you find someone that doesn't like the change you're leading, that is. And you want to know something that's even more difficult than that? Leading change that you don't even believe in for yourself. Yep, I said it. Why? Because we've all been there. If you have been in leadership for any length of time, you've had to stand behind something that you didn't even want simply because it was required of you based on the position you held. Not every time do we feel as passionate and optimistic about change as our superior does. Perhaps your leader didn't pick a solution you thought was best or maybe you didn't even have a say in the matter, you were just told how it is and to do it. Both of these are like being stuck between a rock and a hard place. If you didn't catch the joke - it's just a tough place to be.

How do you lead when there's change that you disagree with or don't think should happen?

How do you lead when there is pushback from other team members, whether you like the change or not?

These are both very difficult places to lead from, but they are both places that, as a leader, you need to learn how to lead through. Your reaction and response in leading change is crucial to how others will follow suit. As a leader, you have a right to an opinion and to oppose change. On that same note, not everything that you have a right to is beneficial.

The Apostle Paul gave this timeless advice to the Corinthian Church in his first letter to them: *"all things are lawful for me - but not all things are helpful"* (1 Corinthians 10:23 NKJV). In other words, just because you have a right to do something, doesn't necessarily mean it's beneficial for you to actually do it. There are many things that are lawful and within your right to do, but aren't beneficial.

It's lawful for you to sit on the couch all day and eat junk food non-stop, but it's not beneficial.

It's lawful for you to scroll on social media for hours at a time, but it's not beneficial.

It's lawful for you to be argumentative and be testy with others, but it's not beneficial.

It's lawful for you to be late to work on a regular basis, but it's not beneficial.

It's lawful for you to express to your staff, co-workers, members, and the public how much you oppose a decision your leader made, but it's not beneficial.

Part 3

Every single one of these scenarios were lawful and gave you the perfect right to act as you wish to act, but none of these scenarios would have been beneficial to you or anyone else. Any decision that we make doesn't only affect us, but will affect those around us as well. It's a selfish thought to think our choices only affect us. This is also true for leading change that you disagree with or don't think should happen. When leading others and serving under a superior, we must learn how to lead even when we don't like the instructions we've been given.

Leading Conflicting Change

As I said before, chances are pretty high that you've had to lead change you didn't like. If that hasn't happened quite yet, just put your seatbelt on and wait a little while, because it will sooner or later. Perhaps you haven't yet, but you already know things aren't going in the direction you would like them to. I want to take you through some tips and thoughts that have helped me in seasons of leading change that I didn't like. I hope that it will help you as it has me.

Examine your feelings

Our feelings are a repercussion of what is happening within us, to us or around us. They are often produced instantly. Most of the time, we have a right to feel the way that we do - but, as we know, that doesn't mean it's beneficial.

When leading conflicting change, the first thing you need to do is understand that

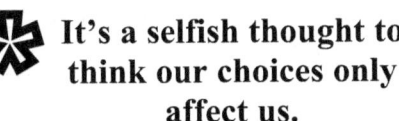 **It's a selfish thought to think our choices only affect us.**

you feel the way you feel for a reason. What is causing this negative feeling? Why is there conflict within you? Once you determine the root, you can know what to do with it. If you feel the way you do for reasons that you shouldn't, that's going to require a lot more soul searching and guidance than what I can provide in this book. But I will say this - if you are in a place where you are having negative feelings about change for reasons that you know you shouldn't be, my assumption is that your feelings probably have little to do with the change and more to do with something else. Regardless, you will need to get down to the root of the matter

Part 3

and attack the situation from there before you will ever be able to get past your feelings.

If your negative feelings toward the change truly is because of legitimate concerns and reasons, then it's likely your feelings are coming from a pure heart that only wants the best for the organization. Not to say that having negative feelings for any other reason means that you don't want what's best, but often times we simply allow our emotions to get in the way of progress.

The Apostle Paul provides us with loads of wisdom like what we read in 1 Corinthians earlier. But we find that he also battled his fair share of wars inside his mind. This is what he tells us in Romans 7:15-24:

For I do not understand my own actions. For I do not do what I want, but I do the very thing I hate. Now if I do what I do not want, I agree with the law, that it is good. So now it is no longer I who do it, but sin that dwells within me. For I know that nothing good dwells in me, that is, in my flesh.

For I have the desire to do what is right, but not the ability to carry it out. For I do not do the good I want, but the evil I do not want is what I keep on doing. Now if I do what I do not want, it is no longer I who do it, but sin that dwells within me.

So I find it to be a law that when I want to do right, evil lies close at hand. For I delight in the law of God, in my inner being, but I see in my members another law waging war against the law of my mind and making me captive to the law of sin that dwells in my members. Wretched man that I am! Who will deliver me from this body of death?

Now, I don't know about you, but that doesn't really sound to me like someone who has a whole lot of control over his thoughts and emotions. In fact, he sounds pretty unstable. *For I do not understand my own actions. For I do not do what I want, but I do the very thing I hate.* Shnikes, Batman.

Part 3

If we were to be honest, though, that's probably exactly how most of us are in a lot of situations in life. We don't know why we do the things we do or why we feel the ways that we feel. What we want to do, we don't. And what we don't want to do, we do. How we want to feel, we don't. And how we don't want to feel, we do.

Why do I have to be this way? you've probably often thought to yourself. I know I have found myself asking that question far too often. Thankfully, Paul answers that question for us, *Now if I do what I do not want, it is no longer I who do it, but sin that dwells within me.* That's right - the "s" word that no one likes to talk about or read about. When we aren't acting the way we know we should (and even want to), and when we aren't feeling the way we know we should (and even want to), it's the sin nature inside of us that is ruling and needs to be shut up.

This, my friends, is why it's so important to really examine your feelings in moments of feeling ways you don't want to feel or in a way you shouldn't be. Are your feelings coming from a place of appropriate concern and love for the organization or from a place of letting the sin nature rule your thoughts and emotions?

Discuss your feelings with the right people

One of the wisest decisions you will ever make as a leader is determining who you can and can't talk to. Trust me with all confidence and assurance that I have had the joy, pleasure, and honor of learning this one the hard way. If you can figure out who you can trust without a major life lesson being involved, by all means go that route.

Most people can't handle it. They can't handle knowing information others aren't privy to. They can't handle you being completely open and transparent with them. They can't handle the hard truths and the harsh realities. It's just too much for them. Their character can't carry it like you can. You need to learn and discern who can be trusted. Never carry the weight alone on your shoulders. Talk to the right person, express your feelings, and see what their viewpoint is. Ultimately, you still have to lead the change with integrity and honor, but this allows you to express your feelings in the right way and in the right context instead of the wrong way and in the wrong context.

Finding someone to express your feelings to has to be done very cautiously. Know who you labor among. There are some people whose problem isn't what you tell them, it's keeping it to themselves and not sharing it with others. Most likely, the person you need to share your feelings with is going to be someone who is already very close to you, someone who has a good track record with you for keeping information private, has likely shared some personal things with you before, and is probably in a position where they know what it's like to lead and keep information private.

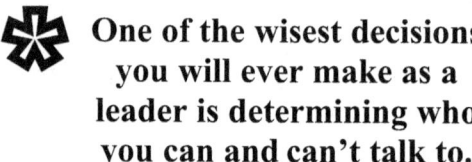 **One of the wisest decisions you will ever make as a leader is determining who you can and can't talk to.**

Minimize the bad

If you have problems with the change, I'm sure you already know all of the reasons why. Most of the time, picking out all the wrong in something comes much easier than picking out all the good. Choose to take the magnifying glass off of these things that are being labeled as *bad*. I'm not saying to be ignorant of the bad to the point where you're being neglectful and in a state of having your head in the clouds (or sand, depending on what kind of landscape you prefer to find yourself in).

Instead, I'm saying to choose not to let the bad be ruler. There are going to be good and bad in every decision, scenario, and change that is ever made. Sure, you hope the good will outweigh the bad, but it can only outweigh if you let it. Often times, we need to re-focus our lens and get our eyes back on the big picture. If you will re-focus yourself and determine in your mind that you aren't going to get caught up on the bad, you will be a much happier individual! Again, I'm not saying to ignore the fact the bad is there, I'm just saying to acknowledge that the bad isn't the only thing present in the picture - there's plenty of good if you will look!

Hype the good

As you're focusing off of the bad, you have to re-focus back to the good. We both know that you already have a list of all the bad stored in your brain, so now why not make a list of all the good? Seriously. Take a few minutes and make a list of all the positives that will come out of this change that you're leading.

Now start thinking about those things and choose to hype those up! Even if you have to force yourself to get hype about it and you're just faking it until you make it. Eventually, you'll get to the point where you're excited about these changes too and you'll be leading with a new perspective. The bad is still very much present, but now we're leading from a different posture. A posture that can lead others the way your called to do.

Zach, you're just sounding crazy now. It's not that easy! Yeah, yeah, I hear you. And I honestly don't disagree with you. But if you will take this advice for what it truly is, it might actually help you. Remember, there are people depending on you!

Trust the decision

Let's just be completely honest with ourselves and realize that not every time we are leading conflicting change will we be able to abide by the first four tips and suddenly have a change of heart as you walk through rays of sunshine and a garden of incredibly scented flowers. As much as we can all probably agree we wish it were this easy, it's just not always going to happen like that. Many times you will find yourself still not liking the change that is coming, no matter how bad you wish you did. This is where it comes down to trust. It's in this moment that you very simply have to trust your leader and trust they are making the best decision. You weren't placed in the position to make the final call; therefore, you have no other option but to trust the person who does.

Leading conflicting change is undoubtedly more of a mind game than it is anything else. In fact, some of the most frequent and most difficult wars you will ever fight are in the battlefield of your mind. The reason they can be the most difficult to win is because you can't overcome using man-made weapons. I believe, though, that if you will use these tips I have given you, they will help you as you lead this change. This isn't to say you're suddenly going to love the change or even agree with it, but I have no doubt that it will help you as you navigate through it.

One other thought that I will leave with you before we move forward is this: while you may not agree with the decision your leader has made for various reasons, there's likely information that you're not aware of and reasons for the decision that your

 It's in this moment that you very simply have to trust your leader and trust they are making the best decision.

leader hasn't shared with you or others. In most situations, not all information behind a decision is going to be revealed. This isn't secrecy, it's merely wisdom. As you are leading change and following under your leader, keep this in mind as well. Again, it comes down to simply trusting your leader.

When You're Not the Problem

But what do you do when it's not you, but rather other people who are against the change? What if it's other staff members, volunteers, members, and co-workers that are giving you pushback? What do you do then?

To start off with, I would give those individuals the same tips and tricks that I just gave you. If they are genuinely trying to be a positive force within the organization, they will take the advice. If they are more concerned about causing trouble, they won't. I'm not trying to be harsh here, but that is the simple truth. Often times it is in the seasons of change in an organization that you start to see people's true colors coming out. You will quickly find out who is really for you and who isn't.

Imitate Me

The next piece of advice I would give you as you are experiencing pushback from others is simply this: just lead. Yep, that's right. Read that again, and then read it one more time. Just lead.

The Apostle Paul, who is seemingly becoming a large focus of this chapter, once wrote these words in a letter to the Corinthian Church, "*imitate me, just as I also imitate Christ,*" (1 Corinthians 11:1 NKJV). I'll be the first to admit this probably sounds a little bit egotistical, doesn't it? But you have to see the heart of Paul before you can receive what he is saying. Paul wasn't trying to be their god or idol. Paul saw a church who was new in the faith and struggling to find their way. But, Paul, being strong in the faith, knew that if they would trust his leadership and character, they would become strong in the faith, too. Paul spent his life following after Jesus and living his life as close to a reflection of Him as he could. This is why Paul essentially said, *if you will imitate me, as I imitate Christ, you will be like the Father also.*

Some of the greatest change that happens among those you are leading in your organization will likely come from imitating you and doing as you do. You have earned trust and confidence among those whom you lead and they will likely follow suit after you. This certainly won't always be the case, but most of the time it will be. If not at first, eventually. This is why I say: *just lead.* If you will simply lead as you would in any other situation, others will see how you are leading and follow after you.

I'm sure that neither you or I come anywhere close to comparing to the man Paul was, but one thing is for sure - we have been given a sphere of influence to be entrusted with. How we lead these people matters.

Leading during conflicting change is not a time for letting others know how much you disagree with the change and what kind of problems it's going to bring with it.

Leading during conflicting change is a time for leadership. A good leader doesn't lead its followers down a path that causes everyone to get separated. Sharing your negative opinions about the change will only cause a divide among the group - leaving one group of people over here and another group **Some of the greatest change that happens among those you are leading in your organization will likely come from imitating you and doing as you do.** of people over there. One group will be excited and in tune with where the organization is going, and another group will be fighting back and disengaged from where the organization is going. The end result - chaos and dysfunction. And here is the most important reality of it all - that end result falls mostly, if not completely, on you, as the leader.

Part 3

Beyond that, the fact of the matter is that you should be leading no matter what. Even if you weren't given the task of leading change in the organization, you should still be leading. As a leader, as someone who has influence, you don't get to hit the off switch or clock out of leading. If there are people around you, you're leading. Why? Because people are following. If you haven't been tasked with leading this change, take it as an opportunity to rally behind the leader who is and support them in what they are doing. This world and your organization needs far less people who enjoy stirring the pot and far more people who will get behind their leader.

A few years ago, the church that I currently serve at was going through an exciting renovation project in our sanctuary. At that point, nearly every other part of our building had been renovated and updated - the sanctuary was the last part of the building that needed some help. The lighting was bad, the projectors and screens were bad, and the carpet and pews featured the most hideous shade of pink you have ever seen. I think we can all agree pink shouldn't go on carpet or pews. Can I get an *amen*?

The sanctuary needed some help, to say the least. And, it was finally getting it. Everyone was more than excited to finally have an updated sanctuary to match the rest of our beautiful and modernized facility. Until some of the pews got re-arranged, that is. Let me explain.

In the old setup of the sanctuary, there were a couple of pews that sat on the far left side of the stage. This was mostly because of a lack of room on the sanctuary floor and the extra pews for seating were necessary. It was less than ideal, but there weren't any other options. However, during the renovation of the sanctuary, some things were able to be moved around and adjusted so that pews would no longer be needed on the sanctuary (thank goodness!), and we could have plenty of seating on the sanctuary floor. This was a much better solution and far more ideal situation than before, no doubt about it.

However, there was an older individual who always sat in a pew on the stage that wasn't quite as excited about this new change. What their reasoning was for being upset was, I'm not entirely sure. What I do know is once they walked into the new sanctuary, the first thing they realized was there was no longer a seat for them on the stage and they weren't happy about it. They proceeded to take off one of the "Reserved" signs attached to a seat that was meant for a Camera Operator and threw it down on the ground while yelling, "I don't care if it's reserved, that's my seat!".

Lesson learned in ministry: people are funny about where they sit. I wish I knew why, but they are. Sometimes change can bring out something in people you didn't even know existed. Perhaps they didn't even know it existed.

Once this individual had time to calm down and really assess the situation, all was just fine and they were able to find themselves a

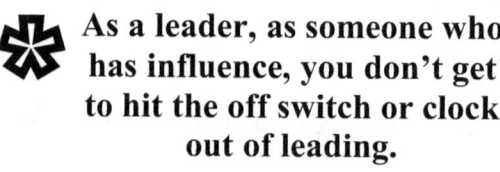 **As a leader, as someone who has influence, you don't get to hit the off switch or clock out of leading.**

new seat to sit in. My guess is they probably did what my first bit of advice was in this chapter and examined their feelings to really figure out why they felt the way they did. Once they realized they reacted in an irrational way, they were able to proceed with more appropriate actions. Truth is - they actually love the new sanctuary and would probably tell you over and over again how ashamed they were of reacting in the way they did. Often times, we react before we even take a moment to examine our feelings, which leads to conflict.

Leading conflicting change is a whole new ballgame and brings different challenges than when you are leading change that majority are in agreement with and are excited about. Unfortunately, nearly all change will bring some level of conflict with it. Rarely will you have the pleasure of leading change with zero conflict. Even if it's something as small as someone throwing a *Reserved* sign on the floor and you have a Camera Operator not really sure where to sit.

Nonetheless, there will always be some change that comes with much more resistance than others. This is the change that we must especially be prepared to lead and lead well. Are you ready for it?

Part 3

Ten

Engage with Change

In case you were wondering - yes, this is where the fun truly
begins! You have theoretically set yourself up for success in
engaging with change in your organization and are ready to start
moving forward with the solution that was decided to be the best
fit. There is so much that is still yet to be thought through,
though, so don't get too excited too quickly. Something I
imagine you don't want to do is have this great solution to bring
in to the organization, but due to lack of planning and properly
engaging with change, the solution falls flat on its proverbial
face. And maybe you do too.

Part 3

In order to successfully bring about change, all things need to be thought through - and yes, prayed through. As we all know from my story in the previous chapter, everyone isn't going to respond to change in the same way. You need to be prepared for that. Beyond that, every aspect needs to be planned through so you don't accidentally leave out any important details or leave any cracks unchecked.

For the purposes of this chapter and to help us better cover the most important phases of engaging with change, we are going to use the acronym - PITE.

Plan ➡ Invest ➡ Train ➡ Engage

This isn't just an acronym, it's a process. This means that in order for it to work properly, it must be followed in the order intended. Otherwise, the end results won't be what you thought it would be. Just like with baking, using the proper ingredients, adding them at the correct time, and following the recipe is important to the success and integrity of whatever you're baking. So, think about this like a cake. After all, cake sounds much more pleasant right now. Don't worry, this isn't *The Great British Baking Show*, but there might be some unsuspected challenges along the way. Unfortunately, you're probably not going to make it on national television or get a nicely engraved serving tray to take home with you either. On the flip side, you're about to be making some incredible changes in your organization that may completely reset and redirect it for greater success and impact than you could ever imagine. What you do today will transform your tomorrow.

For overview purposes, take a moment and look at *Figure 1* on the next page. This is a Change Management Model that will help you tremendously as you engage with change. While this model shares slightly different terminology in some instances than we are in PITE, this will be an excellent tool to use and observe as we use PITE to take these principles into greater detail.

Part 3

This is what the model teaches us: first, we need to define some things before we can continue with planning the path forward.

- Clarify roles in change management process
- Clarify what is changing and why
- Identify stakeholders
- Establish project timeframe
- Clarify success measures

Let's take a look at each of these points in greater detail.

Clarify roles in change management process

Since there is likely a team of you that will be working together to bring this change into implementation, it's important that each person on the team knows what their role and scope of authority is. Just like any other team, there should be an organizational flow of authority, responsibility, and role description. The bigger the change being implemented and the size of the organization, the more important this is.

Figure 1[3]

Change Management Model

DEFINE
- Clarify roles in change management process
- Clarify what is changing and why
- Identify stakeholders
- Establish project timeframe
- Clarify success measures

PLAN
- Conduct impact and stakeholder assessments
- Create change and stakeholder engagement plans
- Identify risks and create risk-mitigation plans
- Design plans for communications and training

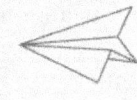

IMPLEMENT
- Enable/activate catalysts and leaders
- Roll out communications and training plans
- Monitor and manage resistance
- Deploy risk-mitigation plans

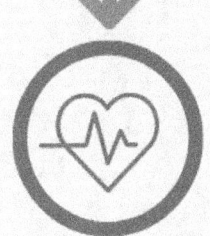

SUSTAIN
- Monitor adoption of change(s)
- Reinforce behaviors that are aligned to the change
- Measure impact of change(s)
- Adjust as needed based on metrics

Part 3

Clarify what is changing and why

Cut to the chase. You and your Change Management Team already knows what's changing and why - but now you need to be able to relay it in layman's terms so that everyone else can understand what is happening and why. They need a simplified version without leaving out any important details. Something that can be explained in short. Figure out what your official statement is going to be and stick to it.

Identify stakeholders

A stakeholder is anyone with interest or concern regarding the matter. Essentially, you need to gather a full list and determine who will be impacted by this change. In other words, who needs to know about this? Check your list and check it five other times. Nothing is more frustrating than being someone who was left out of the loop regarding important and major changes, whether intentional or not.

Establish project timeframe

Be realistic. Is this a change that will be rolled out in phases? If so, how long will each phase last? If it will all happen at once, how long do you hope it will take to see results? Once the announcement regarding the change is communicated, what does the full timeline look like? All of these questions need to be answered and ready to be explained as well as followed as closely as possible.

Clarify success measures

In terms of implementing this change, what do you identify as successful vs. unsuccessful? What problems in the organization are you attempting to alleviate or exonerate through this change? Figure out the answers to those questions and be sure you are able to clearly communicate them when the times comes.

Plan ➡ Invest ➡ Train ➡ Engage

The first phase to engaging with change is to **plan**. Please, for the love of all things good and precious, don't ever try to bring

Part 3

about change in your organization by the seat of your pants.

Your people and your organization deserves better than that. You

are better than that.

So, now that you have defined all of the key information

regarding engaging with the change, you are ready to begin

planning in greater detail. Start off with conducting impact and

stakeholder assessments. In other words, have special meetings

with key people who will be impacted by this change and

determine any roadblocks or issues they foresee occurring during

the transition process. There may be risks they realize quicker or

easier simply because they are working more closely to it and are

the ones working in the field. The knowledge of these people

will be a huge key to a successful transition. You don't want to

miss out on the opportunity to gain insight from them.

Once you have sat down with these key people and

triggered any possible risks or issues that may arise during

transition, then begin to create your change and stakeholder

plans. Meaning, how are you going to move forward with

moving into the transitionary phase of the change? Furthermore,

what are your plans going to be for handling the potential risks or issues that were identified? Having a resolution for these in advance could be detrimental. This is all part of planning and pre-assessed risk-mitigation could arguably be the most important piece in planning.

Finally, you want to design your plans for communications that will be released. This includes any official releases of information to stakeholders, members, staff, volunteers, or even the general public. In addition, you also need to prepare communications relating to any training that will be available and required of stakeholders.

Plan ➡ **Invest** ➡ Train ➡ Engage

The second phase is to **invest**. Once you have made all appropriate preparations in planning for the change, you are ready to actually begin making the necessary investments that are needed to proceed with the transition. This may entail purchasing any equipment or supplies required for the change, as well as any investments needed for training and material. Begin setting these things into motion and purchasing everything that is needed.

Part 3

Plan ➡ Invest ➡ **Train** ➡ Engage

The third phase is to **train**. Before you implement change, you need to be sure that your stakeholders are trained and have been communicated to appropriately regarding these changes. Effective training is vital to successfully leading change. Without properly training your stakeholders, you may as well go ahead and plan for it to fail.

Gagné's Nine Events of Instruction

In 1965, Robert Gagné proposed a series of events that are associated with and address the mental conditions for learning. Without these nine events occurring, an individual's learning will be incomplete or even nonexistent.

1. Gain attention of students

Ensure the learners are ready to learn and participate in activities by presenting a stimulus to capture their attention.

There are a few methods for capturing learners' attention:

- Ask a thought-provoking question

- Lead an ice breaker activity

- Tell a story

- Extremes of emotion

2. Inform students of the objectives

Inform students of the objectives or outcomes for the training and individual lessons to help them understand what they are expected to learn and do. Provide objectives before instruction begins. Tell them in advance what they will be learning about and what they should generally know by the end. Although often accomplished this way, this doesn't necessarily mean bullet points of the objectives are needed.

3. Stimulate recall of prior learning

Help students make sense of new information be relating it to something they already know or something they have already experienced. This could be done by reminding them what the current SOP (Standard Operating Procedure) is, or helping them recall the current problem that is being resolved.

Part 3

4. Present the content

Use strategies to present and cue lesson content to provide more effective instruction. Organize and group content in meaningful ways, and provide explanations after demonstrations.

5. Provide learning guidance

Advise students of strategies to aid them in learning content and of any additional resources that may be available. In other words, help them learn how to learn. Give examples of what to do, and what not to do - what's correct and what's not. Visual aides are always a huge plus!

6. Elicit performance

Have students apply what they have learned to reinforce new skills and knowledge and to confirm correct understanding of concepts. In other words, provide ways they can practice their newly formed knowledge before they are placed in a real world scenario. This could be through effective tests or quizzes, a project, presentation, or any other deep-learning activity or questions.

7.   Provide feedback

Provide timely feedback of performance to assess and facilitate

learning and to allow them to identify gaps in understanding

before its too late. You don't want them to leave their training

session thinking they have a full understanding and knowledge

base regarding the change, only to realize weeks or months down

the road they have been performing incorrectly.

8.   Assess performance

Test whether the expected learning outcomes have been achieved

compared to the training objectives. This could be accomplished

through a post-assessment, embed formative assessments

throughout the training, or crafting other assignments, projects,

or presentations to follow up the training.

9.   Enhance retention and transfer

Help learning retain more information by providing them

opportunities to connect training concepts to potential real-world

applications. Avoid isolating course content, but instead use

previously known concepts and build upon that. Have them

convert information already known into what is now the new reality - *(this is what we used to do, but now we do this).*

According to Gagné, these nine events are crucial to effective learning - and is largely followed in Instructional Design processes in the world today. If you want to effectively train your stakeholders and ensure they are engaging with the change in the way they should so that it accomplishes what it was meant to, I encourage you to study these Nine Events deeper and use them as your guide to creating training material.

Plan ➡ Invest ➡ Train ➡ **Engage**

Finally - and officially - you are ready to engage with change! Once you have made all preparations leading up to this point, it's time to follow the timeline that you created and move forward with leading change. I'm not sure how long of a process this has already been for you or how long you still have until completion, but congratulations! What you are doing in your organization will affect so many lives (hopefully for the better), and I have no doubt it's something you have spent much time in prayer over and is a passion for you. As long as you are passionate about it, you'll be able to get your team behind you and passionate about it as well.

I will be the first to let you know, although I'm sure you already realize, that there will be bumps in the road and everything isn't going to go as planned. There are going to be people who don't like the change and will be sure to let you know about it. There will be things happen that you didn't foresee, and there will be costs you didn't plan on. But, if this change is truly a "God change", you led the way as a true leader should, and you did all of the right things - it will be a success. It may take some time and a little bit of working through some things, but you will get there.

One of the key virtues you're going to need during this transition is probably going to be patience. Patience for a lot of things. Patience for your team to finally get it right. Patience for your members to get adjusted. Patience for all the wrinkles to get ironed out. Ahh, how we so love the word *patience*. Over time, though, your team will finally get it right, your members will get

adjusted, and the wrinkles will all be ironed out.

Meditate to Learn

I'll end this chapter with one quick example, but I will apologize

and warn you in advance that I'm about to gross you out. I

promise it's for your own benefit.

Joshua 1:8 (NKJV) says,

> *This Book of the Law shall not depart from your*
>
> *mouth, but you shall meditate in it day and night,*
>
> *that you may observe to do according to all that*
>
> *is written in it. For then you will make your way*
>
> *prosperous, and then you will have good success.*

Look at the word *meditate*. We find God telling us to meditate

on the Word at least eight different times throughout Scripture.

The word meditate in these verses is actually the same word

ruminate. At this point you're probably wondering, what does ruminate mean? Rumination is what cows do with their cud - their partly digested food. (Oh yeah - I forgot to tell you. This is where things start to get gross.)

This is what happens: cows will get a mouthful of grass (food), chew on it partially, then swallow it. Then, they throw it back up in their mouths, chew on it some more, and swallow it again. And again. And again.

They are ruminating. They are taking something, chewing on it for a bit, let it digest and sit there for a little bit, then bring it back to chew on it again. This is the idea behind meditate. Meditating is taking a thought, thinking (chewing) on it for a little bit, and then swallowing it to let it digest for a bit. Then, later on, bringing that thought back to our remembrance once again so that we can think about it again and in more depth.

The question at this point (for me anyways), is why do cows ruminate on their cud? Not only is it disgusting, but what's the point? Because doing so allows them to get the most nutrients possible out of what they are eating. The same would be true for meditating on the Word of God. And the same is also true for training individuals on something new that you want

Part 3

them remember. If you want them to learn, grow, and truly leave having gained something from your training, you need to teach them how to ruminate their cud. Maybe explain it a little bit less disgusting way, or maybe not. Because I guarantee you this - just like Gagné's First Event of Instruction, if you tell them a story like I just told you, there's no doubt they are going to remember it and you will most definitely have their attention! Likewise, the more that your team is in the field and putting these new practices into use, the better they will get at it. It's going to take some time, but the more they chew on it, the more nutrients they are going to get out of it.

An old quote, whom I'm not sure who to give credit to, says this, "Watch your thoughts, they become your words; watch your words, they become your actions; watch your actions, they become your habits; watch your habits, they become your character; watch your character, it becomes your destiny."

As time will have it, thoughts will slowly but eventually turn into your destiny. This can be both good and bad. This is why it's important to form proper and correct thoughts - to take every thought captive. To have control of what you allow your brain to process and to throw away the bad and incorrect thoughts. We have to train our minds and the more we ruminate and meditate on the right thoughts, our end result (destiny) will be formed the way we desire for it to be.

Part 3

Eleven

Sustaining Change

I was recently asked to help pilot a new system that my

organization would soon be implementing in the months ahead.

It would be replacing the current system, and hopefully, it was

for the better. They asked if I would attend a training session

they had curated for this new system, that would also be the

training used for the organization at large once it was rolled out.

I attended the training and began using the system for about a

month before it was released to everyone else. I gave my

Part 3

thoughts on the training material as well as the new system as a whole.

A week or so went by, and I came into the office one morning knowing that I had a conference call that afternoon with my superior and team. I started off my day as I normally would, working on various different things that needed to be done. But it was a Friday, and Fridays are usually always pretty relaxed and slow. Thank God for Friday.

I was extremely caught off guard, though, when about an hour prior to the team meeting, I received a message from my superior asking if I could lead the new software training during our conference call. She felt that the training provided by the company was poor and left much of the team confused and with a lot of questions remaining unanswered and no easy way to get answers quickly. I calmly and respectfully agreed to the task and then frantically began thinking through how in the world I was going to put together training material in an hour. I didn't have access to any of the company- provided materials at the time, which wasn't very helpful anyway. So, I immediately started brainstorming and putting some stuff together that I thought would be helpful.

If you are wondering whether or not I was able to pull it off - well, of course I was! I wasn't about to fail on such an important task being assigned to me. Not only did the training go well, but next the thing I know, I'm getting another message from my superior. She said she was talking with some of the other superiors and asked if she could share my contact information with them. By the end of the day, I had five other training sessions scheduled where I would be training teams on how to use this new system!

All of this is part of sustainability. Sometimes you will see that your team isn't adjusting to the change in the way you had hoped and allotted for to keep on schedule in transition. This may mean an additional, and perhaps re-invented, training session may be necessary. In this case, there clearly was something that was left out, not enforced well enough, or not communicated effectively during the initial training. In my case, there were a number of teams within the organization who felt like they were still left in the dark and in utter confusion about a lot of things regarding the use of this new system. As some of my superiors were monitoring the adoption of changes, they saw this was a need and asked me if I could provide additional training.

As you begin monitoring the adoption of changes, you may see a lot of different things. The hope is that movement is in a positive direction and staying within the schedule you established for the transition. If this is the case, it's appropriate and necessary to reinforce behaviors that are aligned to the change. If you see that certain individuals, groups, or teams are aligning their actions to the change well then be sure to reinforce that behavior to them. It's not only the right thing to do; it's also psychologically proven to be effective.

Psychology has always been one of my favorite subjects to study in school. I hate to brag, but I always left with an A in Psychology classes. Anyways, studying the response and behavior in individuals and animals has taught us a whole lot.

Positive Reinforcement is a concept in the study of Psychology that can be used to help teach and strengthen behaviors. It can be used in formally training someone or even just naturally in everyday situations. Positive Reinforcement involves reinforcing a stimulus followed by a behavior that will likely occur again in the future. When a positive outcome, event, or reward occurs after a desired action, that particular response or behavior will be strengthened.

Let me use this as an example. Do you remember our story of Bailey the dog in an earlier chapter? The reason Bailey never went outside of the yard was because when he did he was shocked by the electric fence that was once there. Going out of the yard was associated with getting shocked. Bailey didn't like getting shocked very much, therefore he didn't try going outside the fence. Although the electric fence doesn't work anymore and the shock will no longer be received, he still doesn't go outside the yard because he's still afraid he will get shocked (not knowing the fence doesn't work, of course). This is an example of Negative Reinforcement.

The opposite of that would be Positive Reinforcement. Let's imagine that Bailey's owners are out in the front yard trying to teach him how to play catch. They throw a dog bone across the yard and Bailey goes dashing through the yard, grabs the dog bone in his mouth, and runs as fast as he can to take it back to Mom and Dad. Since Bailey was such a good boy and did just like he was taught to do, they give him a treat and lots of back rubs, which are his favorite! They saw a positive and desired action, therefore they approved / reinforced that action with affirmation and a special treat. Bailey now associates going and getting his bone while playing catch with getting treats and back rubs. Now he wants to do that all of the time!

As a leader, we must learn to effectively use Positive Reinforcement among our teams as well. Reinforce behaviors that are aligned to the change. Again, Positive Reinforcement involves reinforcing a stimulus followed by a behavior that will likely occur again in the future. When a positive outcome, event, or reward occurs after a desired action, that particular response or behavior will be strengthened. Therefore, when you see a desired action occurring, and you see that change is being adjusted to and new processes are being followed well, these actions should be followed by a positive event or reward. A simple heart-felt expression of gratitude can go a long way! Beyond that, think creatively of ways to continue reinforcement.

Perhaps as certain goals are being met, a team party can be hosted to celebrate. Maybe there's extra money in the budget for a bonus. Think of gifts that could be given out to express your appreciation.

Reinforce behaviors that are aligned to the change.

Again, none of these things are required, and yes, "thank you" goes a very long way compared to nothing. Whatever you do, be sure that you do something. Never, absolutely never, think and assume your team knows how much you see their hard work and appreciate them. Even if they do know (hopefully they do), make sure they hear it from you often.

Desired Action + Positive Reinforcement = Continued Desired Action

Measure Impact

Next, you want to be sure that you are measuring the impact of change. Before you moved into the transition phase, you assessed any risks that perceivably may occur and should have also created risk-mitigation plans for when they happened as expected. What has the impact of the change been? Has it been more negatively impactful than anticipated or has it been more smooth than expected? Maybe it's nearly spot on to what you thought it would be. Furthermore, is the change as effective as you planned for it to be? Is it correcting the problem you were attempting to solve? What other problems are occurring with the new solution in place? All of these aspects should be evaluated and observed.

According to Prosci, a Change Management Advisor, there are a number of ways you can measure change management:

- Employee readiness assessment results
- Employee engagement, buy-in, and participation measures
- Communication effectiveness
- Employee feedback
- Employee satisfaction survey results

- Training participation, tests, and effectiveness measures

- Usage and utilization reports

- Compliance and adherence reports

- Internal help desk metrics, such as tickets solved, tickets reopened, ticket escalations, issues by resolution area, as well as incidents and problems

- Observations of behavioral change

- Project KPI (Key Performance Indicators) measurements

- Benefit realization and ROI (Return on Investment)

- Adherence to timeline

Many of you are likely reading these suggestions and thinking to yourself how unnecessary all of this is in your context. Truth be told, not all of these will be useful or appropriate in your context. However, I know we will all agree that leading change only to have no concern whether it made any difference would be foolish. If you didn't care what the end result was, why even bother leading change in the first place? Save yourself and keep things the way they are. So, I know you must care about the results of the change. If you truly care, you will put steps into place to be able to measure the impact being made by change and determine the effectiveness of it.

The Flywheel Effect

Finally, as you continue to progress, make adjustments, give positive reinforcement, measure impact, and make some more adjustments, you will eventually get to the point where things are operating as they should be. You've likely heard of Psychologist Bruce Tuckman's memorable phrase, "forming, storming, norming, performing, and adjourning", where he describes the path teams often take in their journey to high performance. At this point in your transition, you should be transitioning into the *performing* stage where the team is flowing and performing at its full potential, and achieving the goals set before them. I'm not really here to talk about these stages, although looking these up would make for a really good assignment for later. However, what I do want to tell you about is the Flywheel effect.

Jim Collins shares of this concept in his book *Good to Great*[4]:

> Picture a huge, heavy flywheel—a massive metal disk mounted horizontally on an axle, about 30 feet in diameter, 2 feet thick, and weighing about 5,000 pounds. Now imagine that your task is to get the flywheel rotating on the axle as fast and long as possible. Pushing with great effort, you get the flywheel to inch forward, moving almost imperceptibly at first. You keep pushing and, after two or three hours of persistent effort, you get the flywheel to complete one entire turn. You keep pushing, and the flywheel begins to move a bit faster, and with continued great effort, you move it around a second rotation. You keep pushing in a consistent direction. Three turns ... four ... five ... six ... the flywheel builds up speed ... seven ... eight ... you keep pushing ... nine ... ten ... it builds momentum ...

eleven ... twelve ... moving faster with each turn ... twenty ... thirty ... fifty ... a hundred.

Then, at some point—breakthrough! The momentum of the thing kicks in in your favor, hurling the flywheel forward, turn after turn ... whoosh! ... its own heavy weight working for you. You're pushing no harder than during the first rotation, but the flywheel goes faster and faster. Each turn of the flywheel builds upon work done earlier, compounding your investment of effort. A thousand times faster, then ten thousand, then a hundred thousand. The huge heavy disk flies forward, with almost unstoppable momentum.

Now suppose someone came along and asked, "What was the one big push that caused this thing to go so fast?" You wouldn't be able to answer; it's just a nonsensical question. Was it the first push? The second? The fifth? The hundredth? No! It was *all* of them added together in an overall accumulation of effort applied in a consistent direction. Some pushes may have been bigger than others, but any single heave—no matter how large—reflects a small fraction of the entire cumulative effect upon the flywheel. ... Here's what's important. We've allowed the way transitions look from the *outside* to drive our perception of what they must feel like to those going through them on the *inside.* From the outside, they look like dramatic, almost revolutionary breakthroughs. But from the inside, they *feel* completely different, more like an organic development process.

Picture an egg just sitting there. No one pays it much attention until, one day, the egg cracks open and out jumps a chicken! All the major magazines and newspapers jump on the event, writing feature stories—"The Transformation of Egg to Chicken!" "The Remarkable Revolution of the Egg!" "Stunning Turnaround at Egg!"—as if the egg had undergone some overnight metamorphosis, radically altering itself into a chicken. But what does it look like from the chicken's point of view? It's a completely different story. While the world ignored this dormant-looking egg, the chicken was evolving, growing, developing, incubating. From the chicken's point of view, cracking the egg is simply one more step in a long chain of steps leading up to that moment—a big step, to be sure, but hardly the radical, single-step transformation it looks like to those watching from outside the egg. It's a silly analogy, granted. But I'm using it to highlight a very important finding from our research. We kept thinking that we'd find "the one big thing," the miracle moment that defined breakthrough. We even pushed for it in our interviews. But the good-to-great executives simply could not pinpoint a single key event or moment in time that exemplified the transition.

We found a very different pattern at the comparison companies. Instead of a quiet, deliberate process of figuring out what needed to be done and then simply doing it, the comparison companies frequently launched new programs—often with great fanfare and hoopla aimed at "motivating the troops"—only to see the programs fail to produce sustained results. They sought the single defining action, the grand program, the one killer innovation, the miracle moment that would allow them to skip the arduous buildup stage and jump right to breakthrough. They would push the flywheel in one direction, then stop, change course, and throw it in a new direction—and then they would stop, change course, and throw it into yet another direction. After years of lurching back and forth, the comparison companies failed to build sustained momentum and fell instead into what we came to call the doom loop.

Part 3

In a nutshell, successful businesses and organizations don't happen overnight with one huge "aha" moment, idea, program, or change. Successful businesses and organizations happen when they build sustained momentum, continually pushing in the same direction with the same amount of force at all times. Change and re-adjustments are okay, but completely changing the course of the organization isn't. It's unsustainable when done repeatedly. If you want to build an organization in your community that truly makes lasting impact and change, build an organization and culture of people who believe in the mission and never stop pushing to make it happen. There's going to be changes made along the way, just make sure that you don't stop pushing. That's sustaining change. That is what will make a difference. That is what will change your community, state, nation, and world.

So, get out there and make a difference today. Be a catalyst for change. You're a world changer and you were born for this.

PART THREE

DISCUSSION

QUESTIONS

1. What is one "go to" tip or trick you always use when giving a presentation?

2. What was the solution that was decided on? What are your thoughts and options about that solution? Why?

Part 3

3. Do you feel this change will cause conflict? What kind?

4. How will you handle any potential conflict? Are you prepared to handle it appropriately?

5. What potential risks do you foresee with this change?

6. In our acronym, PITE, which are you most excited about? Concerned about? Why?

7. What key processes can you use to measure impact

Conclusion

It is truly such an honor that you have decided to pick up this book and read it. I hope that it has been helpful, insightful, and given you nuggets to take and ruminate on. *Sorry, didn't mean to get gross again there!* I hope it has given you something to meditate on. Does that sound better? In all seriousness, my prayer is you are able to take this book and use it as a guide to help you lead change in your personal life, family, friends, ministry, organization, business, or whatever context may be appropriate for you. I genuinely pray it has been a catalyst for change in you so that you can now be a catalyst for change in your organization as you recognize the need for change, find a solution, and engage with change.

You have been given an amazing task that should never be taken lightly. Anytime you have influence among people, you must be careful of every word and action that you do and don't take. Others are looking to us for guidance and leadership. They are looking to us to know what's next and even how to respond to situations as they occur. Be the kind of leader that others would want to follow even if you had no title or position attached to your name. Be the kind of leader that others can rely on and trust to lead with integrity in all situations. They are counting on you.

Being a catalyst for change comes with a lot of responsibility, but the harvest you will reap is plentiful. You have been placed in this position for a reason, and there is so much greatness that can come forth out of a leader who is willing to do whatever it takes to lead change when it's needed the most. The greatest leaders aren't afraid of change - they're afraid of what might happen if they don't change.

I would ask that you consider giving this book to your team members, friends, family, or anyone you believe may be able to benefit from it. This book is all about building strong leaders who know how to identify the need for change, find a solution, and engage with change. This concept is good for far more than the business person - it's good for anyone who may ever just need a change in their life and don't know how to get there.

"The Lord bless you

and keep you;

the Lord make his face shine on you

and be gracious to you;

the Lord turn his face toward you

and give you peace."'

Numbers 6:24-26 (NIV)

NOTES

1 - Kinnaman, David. "The Aging of America's Pastors." *Barna Group*, 2017, www.barna.com/research/aging-americas-pastors/.

2 - *Paul Bloom*, campuspress.yale.edu/paulbloom/.

3 - Shrm. (2021, April 28). *Managing Organizational Change*. SHRM. https://www.shrm.org/resourcesandtools/tools-and-samples/toolkits/pages/managingorganizationalchange.aspx.

4 - Collins, J. C. (2009). The Flywheel Effect. In *Good to great: why some companies make the leap ... and others don't*. essay, Collins.

ABOUT THE AUTHOR

Zach Prewitt is the Associate Pastor & Young Adult Pastor at Newport City Church in Newport, KY. He is an Ordained Minister in the Church of God (Cleveland, TN), where he also serves with his wife on a Young Adult Ministry Committee for the denomination of over 7 million members. In addition, he serves as an Advisory Board Member for Genoa Healthcare (UnitedHealth Group), a Fortune 500 company and America's second largest healthcare company & fifth largest pharmacy chain. He is a graduate of Redemption School of Ministry in Chattanooga, TN where he studied Pastoral Ministry. Together, he and his wife, Sarah, live in Northern Kentucky. Connect with Zach on Facebook, Instagram, Twitter, and at www.zachprewitt.com.

VOLUME I

Good Morning

A MINIMAL DEVOTIONAL

TYLER WOOTEN